AFRICA PRESENTS

THE **CONGO** RDC

AND

TRADITIONAL LAW (*Common law*)

In Bandundu Region (Le Munsong Tribe)

By

BEPONA COLLECTION

AFRICA PRESENTS THE *CONGO* RDC AND *TRADITIONAL*

LAW IN BANDUNDU REGION **(Le Munsong Tribe)**

By

BEPONA COLLECTION

ISBN: 978-0-9859230-0-6

Printed in the United States of America

AFRICA

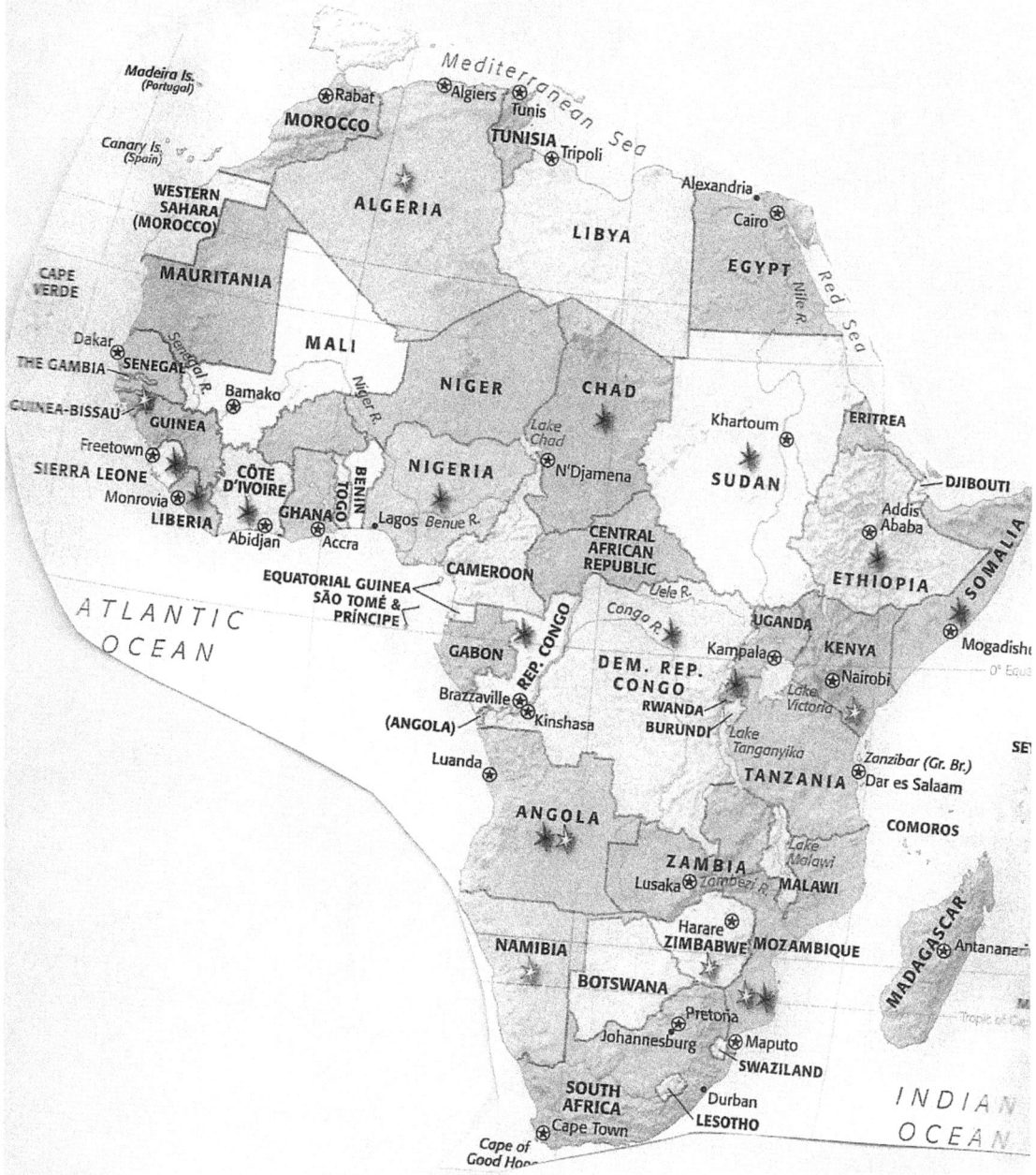

Democratic Republic of the Congo

KINSHASA, *THE CAPITAL CITY OF THE*

CONGO RDC PRIOR TO THE CIVIL WAR

The true knowledge comes from the source.

If I could only learn how to humble myself, and honestly ask from the source the ability and the means of reaching objectives wisely and promptly, I would acquire the wisdom to act and to do right without fear or doubt in a timely manner.

I now realize that the genuine source is "NZAMBE/The Creator of the Universe (Bepona)

African Civil Court, Congolese Style

This open area depicts the official location of Traditional Court in the village.

The villagers are gathered in court. They are awaiting the arrival of Mfumu (Judges) and Mbaku (lawyers) in order to begin the Judgment between a veteran and a shoe repairman who had failed to repair the boot on time. This incident resulted into a serious fight. After listening to the sequence of events followed by questions, answers, and a series of songs associated to each question asked and to the answer given, the verdict is to be given fairly. Naturally, the ruling must always be satisfactory in the eye of their ***Nzambe (uhn-Zambah) or Nzambi-Mpungu (Uhn-Zambe –uhm-Pungu or Mungu*** (God-Almighty, the all knowing), the ancestors, and before all the jurors, as well as the clients involved. The loser of the case gets fined or punished based on the degree of his or her offense. There is no such thing as impunity, corruption, intrigues or treachery involved. Such are the virtues of the African Traditional law.

CONGOLESE TRADITIONAL LAW

THE VILLAGE-CHIEF IN THEIR CASUAL OUTFITS

This picture depicts three village chiefs with their collaborators during an informal discussion where they talk repeatedly regarding the fact that it is vitally important for a native to be anchored in his or her Traditional Law, which is really the only instrument that the ancestors had left us to carry on with the huge legal, social and cultural responsibilities we are now facing. They are reminding each other that Traditional Law is a profound social, cultural and legal instrument that cannot be amended under any circumstances. We have to ensure its integrity as we continue to mourn, grieve and calibrate with the psychological aftermath of war, violence, destruction and illegal exploitation of our resources; which began since the 15th century. This is what has been hindering the new generation to pick itself back up at its every attempt to go forward. In fact, instead of having hindsight, there is nothing but re-occurrence of unnecessary violence. This is why we should not permit any alteration to this instrument. Truly, attempting to instill any item opposite to the virtues of our ancestors would be a fallacy indeed, because such thing would lessen the weight from our ancestors' beliefs.

We do recognize however, that modern law has its place in our modern society; even though, it would never replace the wisdom of our ancestors, which is really imbedded in our hearts, because all those high qualities which we are now evoking, were inspired by our NZAMBE (**unhm-Zambah**)/NZAMBI-Mpungu (**uhn-Zambah-uhm-Pungu**/Mungu, (the titles referring to God, The Almighty, the Great Being in three different Congolese languages.- Lingala, Kikongo, and Swahili). In reality, Traditional Law is based on integrity (fear and respect of the Great Being). And therefore, it is opposite to the terms such as impunity, corruption, or trickery.

707TABLE OF CONTENTS

ACKNOWLEDGMENT

The author and the co-author of this book are both native female Congolese. They had been encouraged by their non-native friends and colleagues who had a yearning desire to know at least one third of the knowledge based on the, "African oral Traditional Law," which is practiced in the African villages, and particularly in the Congo RDC. In addition, this knowledge has never been written before due to its seeming mystery, so to speak. We are indeed grateful to our friends' ardent desire, which has made this book possible.

As far as our dedication is concerned, this book is dedicated to all our loved ones, and especially to those senior clan leaders who have been willing enough to share their knowledge, as well as their past experiences with the younger generation. It is vitally important to learn from those African village chief, as well as the clan leaders in the manner which they proceeded in settling minor as well as serious matters in their society; thereby ensuring integrity, justice, love, loyalty, harmony, peace and respect. The ancient wisdom certainly has helped us to maintain our contemporary oral traditional law. We are grateful indeed for their wisdom of having preserved the ancient knowledge, and had been capable in passing it to their successors immaculately.

Ultimately, this book is written in simple terms, language and style as the readers will actually take notice of it. However, the facts are authentic, ancient and current were all transmitted from the clan leaders' source. They have also been confirmed by our own personal research which was conducted scholarly. And therefore, no bibliography is provided or illustrated from our manuscripts based on "Oral Traditional Law," except to give oral credits to those who deserve it. Finally, for the privacy of some individuals concerned, the exact names of the individuals, as well as the names of their villages are not divulged, due to the confidentiality of the oral traditions. The younger generation should bear in mind that the "Traditional Law" is to remain unmodified.

Central Africa

Democratic Republic of Congo

Traditional Law (in Bandundu Region – Le **Munsong Tribe**)

Introduction

Basically, throughout Africa the Traditional law had always been orally transmitted from one generation to the next, especially in the Bantu/Congolese culture. The information received from the great grandparents is viewed to be genuine, because the source from where it has come is perceived to be actually reliable and viable. The new generation has always accepted the wisdom of their ancestors, as it has been transmitted. And therefore, it would not require any reference in respect to refutation purpose. The Congolese clan leaders had reported that their ancestors' political and social structures had always been impeccable prior to the arrival of foreigners in their land; and they had also been well organized, maintained, and respected.

People were very courteous, refined and always well dressed, according to their social norms. Economically speaking, the currency was always strong and stable. Everyone in the society was encouraged to produce and have a surplus; and that the word shortage and looting were foreign and intolerable to the Congolese society, prior to the arrival of the foreigners' invasions in their land. The leaders were always aware of their responsibilities towards the population, and therefore, they knew how to go about ensuring order and decency as well as establishing an efficient communication with their constituents.

Chapter I

Due to the downfall of the African civilization, which has left a negative impact in many African countries, the Congolese diverse Kingdoms were unfortunately dislocated. They were somewhat scattered, and also badly affected in many ways. Consequently, the most important elements in the Congolese culture as well as those in many African societies were completely lost. Among those lost elements was the African written literature. Nevertheless, the Bantu/Congolese Ancestors like those in many other African societies had maintained their oral literature which the clan leaders continue to pass on to their successors, knowing from their guts' feelings that the ancestors' knowledge should remain unadulterated, because that knowledge is the instrument which the elders utilized in order to maintain peace, harmony, justice and respect around them. Currently, the African new generation relies on their ancestors' wisdom. Ultimately, from that wisdom, originated the "Traditional Law" which the Congolese people refer to with reverence, in Lingala language as "**MIBEKO** (*Mebako*) **Ya** (yah) **Ba** (bah) **KOKO** (coco), meaning ancestors' laws. And in Kikongo language it is referred to as, **NSIKU** (*uhn-seku*) **Ya** (*yah*) **Bambuta** (*ba-uhm-butah*), it means the same as the laws of our ancestors.

Although all the traditional laws have always been orally transmitted, the people continue, however, to preserve their authenticity from generation to generation. This actually is the reason why certain information reported by a non-native is viewed to the natives sometimes, as being fragmentary or colored to some degree, either for a commercial purpose, or just for the lack of accurate information, which leaves a gap in between that might cause repudiation.

Further, at times the information is somewhat amplified intentionally for a commercial purpose as we have previous indicated, or merely for the sake of stigmatizing relevant information of other people.

Occasionally, in communicating with the outsiders, the natives usually suppress certain information which is deemed to remain sacred. In actuality, all the genealogical information is supposed to be orally transmitted in this society. The African new generation receives its information directly from the horses' mouth or from the source, so to speak, and therefore the information, which is originated from a native, is considered to be genuine. In the Bandundu region, for instance, the traditional laws are practiced mostly in the villages by the village chiefs called "Mfumu (*uhm-fumu*)," who actually preside the traditional courts. Mfumu (*uhm-fumu*) worked in collaboration with Mbaku (*uhm-baku*) traditional lawyers, referring to some areas of **Bandundu Province (Luniungu region).** *As we proceed, readers will take notice how these individuals actually conduct the judgment of various cases, in their villages as well as in their local government offices; We will perceive exactly when the villages' Mfumu decide to bridge the trial from Traditional law to our current, or modern law.*

SETTLING DISPUTES In Traditional Court

Basically, whenever the disputes occur between a plaintiff and a defendant, this situation usually happens between the individuals from different families in that particular village. The claimant concerned has to follow a hierarchical procedure prior to seizing the court of law. In the Congolese villages of Bandundu region, for instance, naturally, the plaintiff will file an oral complaint. Primarily, that complaint should be addressed to his or her clan chief; and subsequently, the clan chief would exercise his family's authority. After converging with all his family members, he will then seize the village chief who is generally a male individual. He, in turn will communicate, shortly after that with his colleagues, who are actually the chiefs of the neighboring villages. They are at the same time a part of that local court. Finally, all of them would come together to decide an appropriate day of scheduling the judgment. The local or the village court is actually presided by a group of Mfumu (uhm-fumu) (village rulers) who share equal power from their respective villages. The Congolese ancient societies, as well as many other African societies had no written laws as was previously indicated, but relied on well-defined customs; therefore, all of them are required to honor their ancestors' laws with reverence, because it is regarded as a profound document.

Generally, the village chiefs work in unison in settling the constituents' disputes. However, if the local court fails to settle the matter adequately or fairly, either due to the nature of the case, or because the case had been found to be very complex, or complicated (example: crime case, or any other serious matters), in order to appeal, the trial would have to be transferred to another level of traditional court which is presided by a very high Chief, who had been appointed collectively by the village chiefs of the vicinity. That high level of "Mfumu (uhm-fumu)," is termed as "Grupema (groop-ma)." He is actually viewed as being equivalent to a District Judge or something to that effect. Nevertheless, he is still regarded as a traditional court Judge, because the judgment is, in fact, being still prosecuted on the local or the village level. The only difference however is the fact that the Grupema (high Judge) in the village had been empowered collectively by all the village chiefs of the surrounding area, and therefore, that individual appears majestic compared to the rest of the village Chiefs. The reason he had actually earned that title of honor is due to his highest reputation of settling trials successfully and wisely in his past experience, and also had acquired a sound experience.

CHIEF GRUPEMA'S POWER

The Chief Grupema is regarded as a professional historian who is very knowledgeable of the traditional laws, and had acquired a solid experience in conducting judgment as it was previously indicated. In addition, because of his title, he appears majestic in terms of his dress code, while exercising his duty. He wears a piece of material called "Lepiah" in the bottom, instead of wearing a pair of trousers. Lepiah is made out of a very fine and expensive silk like fabrics, or velvet like material, according to our contemporary clan leaders, Lepiah was made out of Punga-Punga Fibers (resembling to flax-fiber). On his upper part, the Judge Grupema wears a jacket decorated fully with divers gadgets of various colors, usually white, silver and gold.

Further, over his jacket, one would notice sometimes, two diagonal straps crossing from his left shoulder to his right side, precisely, below his right arm. In addition, on his jacket, stand shoulder-straps to prove his authority. Furthermore, the Chief Grupema wears a special hat adorned with different size of white-bullets ornaments. Moreover, he walks with a special cane designed just for him. Brief, his appearance just inspires an honor to the observers.

As was previously mentioned, Chief Grupema is actually a title of honor granted to the most qualified local judge who exhibits a high degree of expertise in the traditional laws.

Usually, a Chief Grupema or the local official has a history of settling the cases successfully, due to his high qualifications, along with his passed outstanding experience. Prior to starting the trial session, upon his arrival in court, the Chief Grupema first confers once more with the other village or local Mfumu (uhm-fumu) in order to have an overview of the matter that is concerned, or the topic which had been scheduled for trial on that particular day (usually on a Sunday.)

In essence, in the villages, a local court is not a building per se, but it is actually an open comfortable shaded area, under beautiful trees, (*see picture page 6)* a place designated to hold a local judgment. Generally, the trial is held on a nice bright afternoon day.   However, should the weather (referring to the rainy day) intervene with the assembly on that day, in that case, the court's schedule would have to be adjourned for the following Sunday. Apparently, if the judgment had been found to be unfair to one of the parties involved, the clan leader of the alleged party would then be compelled to appeal the case, by seizing the local government officials at the Regional Court called, "SECTEUR." This point is actually the beginning of the bridge between the "Traditional Law" and contemporary law. The judges at the local government office are required to have both knowledges of the traditional law, as well as that of our modern law, proficiently in order to be able to conduct the trial wisely. Ultimately, at that level, any party who would be found guilty would be charged with an appropriate penalty; usually, in the form of both finance, and prison in need be. He could be sentenced from six months to two years for his or her offense. *Readers should bear in mind that there is no such thing as impunity, corruption or treachery in the Traditional Court of law.* It is also necessary to indicate that the traditional judgment is composed of *verbal statements* from parties concerned, which are followed up immediately by *audio (singing) statements* from the Mfumu (*uhm-fumu*), or the Mbaku (*uhm-baku or lawyers*) who are conducting the trial. That particular short song should always be sung right after each party's response, and usually one stanza only is permitted to be sung. As a matter of fact, that song should be specifically related to that particular party's statement. *During the trial, the song could actually be initiated by one of the Mfumu (uhm-fumu) or Mbaku (uhm-baku) who has sensed the direction to which the trial is actually being headed.*

Additionally, prior to singing that short and little song in order to back up the party's statement or response, usually, two Mfumu (uhm-fumu) or Mbaku (uhm-baku) would suddenly stand up before the Assembly. And then, both would gaze at each other for a few secondes, as a signal to begin clapping of their hands simultaneously while they are actually singing. And subsequently, the trial would be resumed right afterwards. Furthermore, the type of the song chosen would have to be completed related with the question asked, and the answer given by the plaintiff, or by the defendant. This step is vitally important in settling disputes, or any other mattersr involved in the Congolese villages from Bandundu Province.

In reality, the type of song selected right after the answer received is generally an indication that either the plaintiff or the defendant is actually wining the case, or it could also be another way around. At the cross examination time, it all becomes clear to every party concerned, as well as to all the jury members or witnesses who had gathered in that court, at that particular moment.

Chapter II

BELOW WE WILL EXAMINE THE JUDGMENTS OF VARIOUS CASES
INCLUDING VERDICT GIVEN FOR EACH CASE.

TRIAL OF ADULTEROUS CASE

CASE No. I

How does the Congolese traditional Court handle the judgment of the

unfaithful spouses?

When one of the spouses alleges that his or her partner has been engaged in the adulterous activities, the Mfumu (uhm-fumu/Mbaku (uhm-baku) or the village Judges actually organize a court hearing for both spouses. At the court hearing, the judges would seek proofs or any physical evidence pertaining to such allegation. In the villages, the best means of acquiring any tangible physical evidence of the adulterous case would actually be, by watching the movement of the party suspected in such shameful relationship. Normally, the partner would try to obtain proof by carefully following his or her spouse in the direction where the spouse has been going frequently during that particular period of time. In reality, that would be in the attempt to apprehend the partner who has been cheating or committing the act of adultery.

Generally, this could happen in the forest where the husband and his wife conduct their fields' activities. Effectively, spouses in the villages could have more than one locations from which the couple consider to be the sources of their livelihood. In reality, it could be three different localities such as the forest where they had cultivated their fields, or it could also be in the area where they have fish ponds for the breeding of fish or "pisciculture" activities. Further, it could also be towards the spring water fountain.

Apparently, conducting such an investigation could be tedious to the partner concerned, due to the fact that the partner would have to deal with three alternatives, or locations to carry his or her investigations, in the attempt to come out with any physical evidence. Unfortunately, such procedure happens to be the optimum way of carrying out an investigation related to the unfaithful partner around the villages.

These types of investigations are more applicable to an unfaithful woman rather than to a male partner. However, snooping activities could be very complicated sometimes, but when the partner is determined to have a tangible physical evidence, he or she has to follow the procedures regardless, that is, if he actually desires to unravel the seeming mysteries in order to win the case involved.

Obviously, without any tangible proof, or any physical evidence which the court has required, the judge would feel obligated to dismiss the case; and especially, if the defendant denies the allegation. If one of the partners is however, wise enough, and had suspected the location where the partner had been going consecutively during that particular period of time, this could serve him or her as a clue to attempt his or investigations by following on her or his footsteps. The claimant could take a different approach, if he so desires. He or she may in that case delegate a trustworthy person, either a friend or a relative to follow up on that individual's footsteps in the attempt to catch the individual suspected having an affair. That trustworthy individual would needs to be however bold enough in order to testify in court before the Mfumu (*uhm-fumu or Judges*) honestly, and that person also would have to appear fearlessly in describing the scene involved vividly.

Ultimately, when one of the partners has actually been caught, at that time, the wrongdoer would be judged, based on that physical evidence *according to the law*. The pretender is given two options: either he or she would have to file for a divorce, which is done orally, of course, or forgive and continue to live with the spouse, after having met other court requirements. If, however, the partner decides to forgive the culprit, the court will have to charge him or her a double-portion fine. The fine that is charged is usually paid in form of livestock, such as three goats plus any designated number of containers of traditional wine. If the offense was found to be less serious or minor, the law requires that the fine be paid in the form of fowl, such as chickens, or ducks, plus three containers of palm-trees wine, to the judges. To the alleged partner's family, however, the court would give at least one quarter of the fine.

The judgment of infidelity is usually settled at the village local court, where the Mbaku (*uhm-baku*) village rulers would request a fine of no more than three goats as was previously mentioned, which will be divided in the following manner: Two goats will have to go to the Mfumu (uhm-fumu)/Mbaku (uhm-baku) or the village rulers, including three (3) Nkalu (traditional bottles or containers) of Palm-tree wine. And then, one goat plus one Nkalu (*uhn-kalu*) bottle of Wine will be given to the claimant's family, assuming that he or she has won the case.

However, after the verdict, if one of the partners initiates a divorce in court, at that time, the judgment would have to be adjourned until the next session. The divorce procedure based on the unfaithfulness case, takes longer than any others, because the court is really cautious when handling divorce case; in that regard, the judges would need to systematically follow all the steps involved in the Traditional Law, prior to finalizing the divorce case.

After the court hearing, the Mbaku (uhm-baku) (judges) allow both spouses to wait for a period of six to one year in order to observe whether or not the spouses could consider any reconciliation option. During the waiting period however, both spouses are not permitted to have any physical relationship with any other partners outside of marriage, until the divorce has been finalized. Conversely, if after the set time both husband and wife feel that the possibility of continuing married life is perceived to be completely negative, in that case then, the prosecution to finalize the divorce would be initiated steps by step based on the traditional law.

Both spouses will receive an official oral date in order to appear once again in Court. Usually, the judgments of every case except death are always scheduled on a Sunday afternoon; customarily, it should always be held after the Church worshipping.

Prior to the trial day, however, an oral announcement would be made in order to alert all the villagers to attend the trial. People would be mobilized to witness the divorce judgment in court, on that day and time. Should both spouses maintain their decision for a divorce, the judges will have to accept it; and will give them a set date required in order to finalize the said divorce. The final step of the divorce case in the Congolese society of Bandundu region is ultimately sealed traditionally, by the *"Washing of the Hands Ceremony", this means that* spouses wash each other hands, simultaneously, in front of the assembly in order to indicate that they are officially divorced; but it must be officially sealed by the ultimate step, or the splitting process, which is known as the "Running Away ceremony, which ends their marital status. Once the washing of both spouses' hands is completed. *Please follow the operation carefully below and observe how these s activities occur.*

Thereafter, the judges will order both spouses to operate the **"RUNNING AWAY"** activities from each other. Each one is to run away in an opposite direction, until both of them are no longer in the view of the court officials and all the witnesses. As they are both performing the running away activity, each one must bear in mind that divorcees must not look back while performing the running activities, regardless to what is happening behind them, until each one reaches his or her home. Failure to do so would result to a serious problem for the individual who had violated the law. That individual is actually subject to be penalized by the court.

Finally, after the washing of each other's hands and the running away activities have been performed, the couple can be then considered officially divorced. Formally, they are free to establish any type of relationship with whomever they choose to marry without any further concern, or violation of ancestors' laws.

JUDGMENT OF LARCENOUS CASE
CASE No. II

How Do Traditional Judges settle Larcenous Case?

Based on the traditional laws, robbery is regarded as a *STINKING ACTION, and eventually it appears as an insult to the Bantu/Congolese ancestors' beliefs*.

Theft is an action of disgrace in the eyes of the village Chief and his constituents, as well as in the eyes of the clan leaders. Therefore, the action of **Robbery** is forbidden in the entire villages as far the integrity is concerned. So, the individual who steals or who commits a larcenous offense would have to undergo a severe penalty. And the theft victim would have to accept the consequences of his or her misdeed, which is a shameful ceremony, which really stinks physically and psychologically. *As it will be described further in this chapter*; the punishment reserved to a theft victim had been found to be the optimum punishment, which could actually do justice to such a victim, according to the traditional laws. In fact, the Congolese society, even prior to its being submitted to persistent foreign invasions, and to the warfare which resulted to the activities performed by **"Mundel-A-Bangombe** (*Moon- dal Ah Ba-n – Gom –bah), which means the kidnapping of the Congolese people by foreigners merchants, and impostors)*", as well as to the looting of their goods, the State of Kongo was economically and politically sound at the earlier time, the clan leaders reported that the population had always been self-sufficient. And therefore, the village Chiefs as well as the clan leaders had always encouraged their constituents to be engaged primary in the agriculture activities, then in the fishing or creation of the fish ponds for fish breeding purpose. Additionally, people were engaged in cattle-breeding, hunting, farming, trading as well as producing a variety of other commodities such as pottery of various styles. *People practiced trading of the goods they manufactured and were capable to networking with other countries harmoniously. That actually, was prior to the arrival of the Portuguese or the early catholic missionaries in the Kingdom of the Kongo in the 15th century. The traditional law had revealed that, the practice of African hospitality to a higher degree had permitted the perpetual violence in the land of Kongo. The King of Kongo had lost his ancestors' vision, because he allowed himself to be distracted by the foreigners instead of utilizing Nzambe (uhn-Zambah) or his God given discernment.*

Even though the Bantu/Congolese societies were actually dislocated due to the foreigners' pillage which has left the Congolese villages and their respective families in such a deplorable state, people still held on into their ancestors' traditional law, because that was the only reliable instrument that was left in their possession, eventually it was impossible for anyone to steal it from their minds and hearts.

Based on the norms of the society, each family had always produced a high volume of crops or a surplus. And that had been the reason why each home state had always built a granary (*a warehouse)* in order for the people to store the surplus of their harvest. Therefore, the Congolese society, for decades, had always maintained a surplus image. Such was the reason why "stealing action," was viewed as being foreign to them, because no individual in the society had ever experienced any shortage in regard to the supply required, until at the latter epoch. That was due to the arrival of the envious individuals who were originating from the famine and barbarous societies. Evidently, the influence from the outsiders had brought different people with different cultures, and eventually that integration had created such a negative impact in a refined society. As a result, the Mfumu and the Mbaku of the villages had to develop new measures of punishing larcenous victims without any discrimination, and it was implemented thereafter.

AMBI – STINKING PUNISHMENT

Nevertheless, the village rulers, the clan leaders, and the cream of the crop had to come out with some sort of disciplinary measures of controlling everyone who opted to steal from his or her fellowman, and causing insecurity among the villagers. In order to prevent such a degrading activity, the decision was made to exercise the same type of punishment to every individual who would commit that offense; whether it be a male or a female had to be forced to undergo a severe *STINKING* punishment. Because *STEALING* is actually viewed as a very serious offense, the society perceived it as being, *DREADFUL,* indeed*!* Because, the Traditional law requires that men or women ought to exemplify their commitment to the society in terms of their productivity. They ought to be rewarded based on their own endeavor. The Bantu culture states that a brave man must prove his stamina by his productivity. Though, the man who chooses to steal, instead of working in order to earn his living honestly, is considered to be worthless. He is a traitor to the society, because of his lethargic attitude. This should be regarded as an insult to the ancestors' virtues, which is a violation of the Traditional law. So in order to prevent theft altogether, in some villages of Bandundu region, specifically in Luniungu Sector, the village chiefs had developed a punishment called "*AMBI*," it is also called a **STINKING CEREMONY**. "AMBI" is actually an application of a dirty paste, composed of a few unpleasant stuffs, exuding unpleasant odor, which was designed to paint thoroughly on the theft victim's body for having deliberately, degraded the positive image of the society, which is in reality an awful or a negative influence on the mentality of the younger generation.

The stinking ceremony is to be performed in the village court, before the traditional Judges (Mfumu (*uhm-fumu*) or Mbaku (*uhm-baku*), and it should be done in the presence of all the clan leaders, all the witnesses, as well as the plaintiff and the defendant's families. It is actually mandatory for both families to be present during the ceremony, in order to witness such a degrading scene, for having actually failed to instruct their family member appropriately. *Please bear in mind that the painting of the "Ambi" scene is very embarrassing to the family involved, because the family would have to cope with the psychological aftermath which may result to a negative outcome around the family.*

In effect, while the stuff is being painted on the theft's body, by a special Judge called "*AMBI JUDGE*," the theft victim has to be answering a series of questions – from the Judge operating the ceremony.

Please follow the example, of the thief, Mr. Lundo and the Judge, the moderator.)

Question: (Ambi judge): *Mr. Lundo why are you undergoing this Ambi Ceremony, today?*

Answer: (Theft victim): ***Because stealing STINKS! – JUST LIKE THIS DIRTY PAINT!***

Question: (Ambi Judge) *Mr. Lundo what would you prefer to be doing for the rest of your life in the future? Would you rather be a theft, and be subject to the Ambi penalty consecutively, or you would prefer to be a producer, and gain respect in our society?"*

Answer: (theft victim): ***Never Will I Steal Again From My Fellowman,***" The victim would actually confirm before the observers who came to assist in trial" ***I Will Make Certain to Be a Producer from this day on; and never again would I dare to become a Theft, because such as ceremony is very shameful!"***

At the completion of the application, the victim will be asked to remain seated before the assembly for *One Hour*. And finally, the *AMBI Judge* would order the victim thereafter to stand up, and go to the nearby river. Usually, he must be accompanied by a witness designated to carry the victim's clean clothing with a soap bar in order to clean himself or herself thoroughly, by immersing the entire body in the water. And afterwards, he would join his or her family as a clean individual. He would be considered as a new person, clean emotionally, morally, physically, as well as spiritually. Apparently, the "AMBI" punishment seems to be the most embarrassing ceremony among the others in the society, because the individual actually loses his self-esteem afterwards. Sometimes, it may cause a divorce to some couples for having caused such an embarrassment to his or her partner, unless the partner had participated in that conspiracy.

In effect, the village head issues the warning, and frequently reiterates the village regulations in order to persuade the individuals in remaining focused in the appropriate or positive activities. And therefore to refrain from doing wrong to their fellowman in the attempt to make a living as such action would undervalue you as a person.

So often, the village chief would say to his constituents: "A man should get involved in handling men's responsibilities, and a woman should do likewise. When men and women remain focused in their daily duties, the desire to steal would be eliminated completely. Further, any thought of putting any burdens on another family member, or attempting to envy those who endeavor to produce crops or cattle-breeding or growing of the fish in the fish ponds, must be stopped altogether.

The village Chiefs and the clan leaders make certain that the youth are well trained in those areas since their early days; so that those youth would become self-sufficient as soon as they grow up. They also would be able to raise their own families with a high standard. We do not wish to underestimate anyone in our villages, because our ancestors had told us that everyone, especially our youth are stronger than they appear to be. Therefore, showing them good example would motivate each one to act right around our villages and develop fear of our Nzambi-Mpungu, God in heaven, as our ancestors had said, "Do not mess up with Nzambe, because even the little gods fear Him tremendously." So, if we do not train our youth right, we will have to be the ones to pay the penalty of their disobedience, and their wrong doing.

The male individuals would be incapable to exemplify their African men's stamina; therefore instead of staying power, they would lose that vision and eventually become lethargic. Consequently, they would seek to place their burdens on the rest of their family members, which is unacceptable or unethical. As you understand that the spirit of laziness is associated with an evil desire to do wrong to your fellowman, who works hard to earn the supply needed to provide for their families. This is why the concept of committing any robbery offense cannot prevail in our society. However, Ambi penalty will have to prevail until everyone develops fear and repugnance of such a repulsive ceremony.

Basically, after the performance of a *STINKING CEREMONY* in one village, generally, it would become a pattern to the rest of the village rulers of the neighboring villages. They would be prompted to remind their own people to refrain inappropriate behaviors as well, because they dishonor their ancestors' belief. Further, the youth should be encouraged to honor and respect their society's norms, and refrain from adopting any wrong, foreign culture, which is unsuitable to our society.

They have to become accustomed in doing what our ancestors had done best in order to become self-sufficient; that would of course requires doing physical work such as cultivating crops, farming, fishing, cattle-breeding, trading, and hunting. They actually endeavored earning their living honestly and respectfully. Our ancestors were not just rolling their eyes elsewhere in every direction, north, south, east, and west in the attempt of planning evil against those people who were willing to live harmoniously and maintain their surplus.

Does the Traditional Law Prohibit Asking Help From Neighbors?

Evidently, asking some help or things from a neighbor from time to time, is not prohibited in the Bantu society, because Congolese ancestors believed in Sharing with those around you, and never to be self-centered. That is why parents are recommended to instruct the youth from their younger age in practicing sharing with family members, close friends, as well as with their neighbors, in order to prevent them becoming egotistical. Our ancestors believed that a society filled with self-interested individuals would generate antagonism in place of love. Nevertheless, sharing activities are practiced out of courtesy, and not in the support of lethargic individuals who lack ambitious as such negative conception would destroy the aspiration of the younger generation.

However, people who ask help must bear in mind that it should be done moderately and harmoniously. In fact, those individuals who ask for help should not be doing it perpetually either, as that would demean the image of our society, reiterate the village rulers in that respect.

Ultimately, the village chief would make an inference of the situation after having completed such an appalling Ambi ceremony, and then, he would utter the following words, "Again my people, please do not steal or assault anyone in order to make a living, but work or 'ASK kindly!" Because, looting activities belong to the Barbarous societies. They are truly foreign to our society. The barbarous individuals, in fact, had unfortunately, practiced envious spirit for decades, because they had been exposed to penury in the barbarous world, which is opposite to ours, so they rationalize their deeds in doing so, but we were never accustomed to act violently and we would never permit anyone in our society to duplicate what is not allowed in our traditional law, which is in reality the instrument of integrity.

In essence, individuals who support the wrong notion cannot belong to a respectable, spiritual, and refined society such as ours! Because our ancestors had said, "NZAMBI-MPUNGU (uhn-zam-be –uhm-pun-gu) meaning "God Almighty," had told the people that they must work in order to make a living. He had not told the people that, "You are permitted to rob from your neighbors in order to make a living," the village chief would affirm it repeatedly. He would be stern in reminding his people, "Our ancestors were not acquainted to such thing, and therefore, our society will never adopt it either.

The village head would also assert that Stealing from another part of life (*whether a brother, friend or other*) cannot be *Tolerated in this Society.* **You may ask why not?** *Well, because such dishonorable action is against our Ancestors' Norms; and that is the reason why we refuse to be a part of such perception and encourage everyone to continue evoking our hidden values!" As a village head, my objective is to restore the qualities which had been covered up for decades.*

OFFICIAL COMMUNICATION IN THE VILLAGE
HOW DO VILLAGE CHIEFS COMMUNICATE WITH THEIR CONSTITUENTS?

Since the villages have no radio stations, the village chiefs take the responsibility of announcing any relevant information to their constituents, *"ORALLY."* Generally, the announcement had to be made between the hours of 7:00 p.m. - 8:00 p.m. That is virtually the time everyone is practically at their respective homes, and is also in a relaxed or in a receptive mood. The village chief would walk up and down the village, making the announcement; and reminding the people not to forget that the *"AMBI CEREMONY* prevails and must be sustained so long as individuals choose to misbehave. Although, we extend our hospitality to everyone, however, we do not welcome disrespect to our Tradition Law." *This is what a bright and firm village head would continue to announce sternly.*

Whenever such an event occurs in the vicinity, the *Chief Grupema* would ensure to send his personal message to every nearby village rulers, asserting, "Please take your stand and announce that, 'Anyone who dares to steal, that would entail that such individual has really chosen to dishonor Nzambe, our God the great being in heaven, and also to disrespect the village Chief, as well as all the clan leaders and their respective families, this is culturally wrong.

And therefore, any individual who violates the law of our society would be subject to undergo the severe *"Stinking Punishment"* without fail! In addition, everyone should be made aware that Stealing is also a dishonor even in the eyes of your fellowbeings. Moreover, it is so, especially to the children who must follow after your footsteps." *BRIEF, chief Grupema would ensure to reiterate the followings words:* "THE WORD STEALING STINKS ALTOGETHER, IN CASE YOU WERE NOT AWARE, NOW YOU SHOULD BECOME AWARE OF IT! *Therefore, it should be avoided* completely from the vocabularies of the people of this society once and for all!" Therefore, "Ambi Punishment had to be reinforced, and the law shall not be abrogated or amended until the word theft has been "ERADICATED" completely from this society!"

As a result, to such constant reminder, people would wind up developing a high degree of fear of undergoing such a shameful punishment. In regard to this point, Chief Grupema, would sound redundant, and would reiterate the following: "The Stinking law applies to a male and female alike without any distinction. And therefore, any individual who does not want to be stinking with Ambi paint he would better refrain taking such an awful action!" BECAUSE AMBI STINKS, AND WILL CONTINUE TO STINK AS LONG AS INDIVIDUALS CHOOSE TO STINK!" *Please note, we intentionally choose to sound* REDUNDANT *regarding this matter.*

CLAN LEADER'S ACCOUNTABILITY

Could a Clan Leader be prosecuted for the Misdeed of any of his family members?

The suitable answer to this question would actually be, "yes" he could, because as a rule, the family's leader is held accountable for the misdeed of any one of his family members. Why should it be so? That is according to the Bantu/Congolese culture, the person in command of the family, is supposed to oversee every situation that is occurring in the family cycle, days and nights. He or she should be aware of every activity performed by everyone in the family. Therefore the family leader should actually urge everyone in the family cycle to be productive, except in the case of illness, where every family member is required to provide assistance, until his or her recovery.

Also, as a rule, the clan leaders would recommend or insist on the fact that everyone in the family should really marry within the nearby ethnic groups whose languages and cultural institutions are somewhat similar. In this particular society, people actually believed that marrying within close proximity would facilitate communication in regard to each other's cultures, and would also develop mutual respect of their respective rules and regulations.

Further, the people also believe that the complete knowledge of each other's culture would strengthen families' relationship. And therefore, it would facilitate assisting each party regardless of their remote origins. This fact also would prevent causing any emotional disturbance or creating any unnecessary tension between the parties involved.

Basically, the village Chief would repeatedly, remind his constituents that the individuals who had inter-married with partners who are originated from different and remote backgrounds, or those coming from the country's borders, should really take the responsibilities of explaining essentially everything regarding the norms of the society wherein they have been integrated. In fact, those individuals should also be made aware regarding the restrictions involved within the society. Because, the outsiders do not always have the knowledge of our norms, rules and regulations, and therefore, they are likely to lower the morality of our people, which might undervalue the high standard of our society. And therefore, the Painting of the AMBI substance, due to its strong disgust, shall remain our ideal and optimum "Stealing Penalty." Stinking ceremony shall be in fact applied, even over the body of any newcomer, who has just been integrated in our society, regardless of their duration in our villages.

Regardless to its current appearance, our society still sustains the remnant of its social class composition. The cream of the crop or modest or common people, nevertheless, everyone is a part of our society. Therefore, the newcomers should act accordingly. Apparently, things might not appear as obvious as they had been during our ancestors' time when they were refined, but, to some degree, they are in our hearts. It is understandable for the newcomers to appear awkward, in terms of refinement; apparently, they are not accustomed to hearing this word. Nonetheless, if they are willing to be trained, we can always shape them in the same manner we actually shape our youth.

Apparently, their previous village chiefs and their clan leaders were not accustomed to hearing the word 'REFINEMENT either. And therefore, such word called refinement has no impact in their societies or in the mentality of these new people. How could their chiefs establish any line of conduct for their constituents, if their ancestors did not live or practice it? Since compassion is one of the elements in our Traditional Law, we must take the responsibility of training them so that they could gradually change their peculiar behaviors and adjust to our Bantu/Congolese ethic. Such situations would eventually make the task of a village chief and that of the leaders very difficult to control. Most of the time, their peculiarity would cause disturbance and disobedience to our rules and regulations, if we actually fail to take that stand. Eventually, the presence of those individuals would entail a serious education or training (orally) in order to meet our social standards. The village chiefs would discuss among them, expressing their deep concerns of maintaining the high image of their societies.

The rulers' favorite statement would be in that matter: 'Please train your guests (all the new comers), because the Ambi punishment does not discriminate, as you know, when it comes to the robbery offense.

TRAINING OF NEWCOMERS IN THE SOCIETY

Message from the village chief to those who are associated with individuals from different societies: Please, *advise your guests, tell them, teach them, and show them how they should, in reality live with us here in our society*, which literally has a high respect to our ancestors' norms. In fact, new people in the community should not be taken by surprise; in regard to the penalty associated to stealing activity. We, on the other hand do not which to appear disrespectful either. However, the guests should be made aware that the Ambi penalty does not discriminate. The village Heads would sound sometimes redundant to their constituents, but would continue to do so in order to make their authority felt, and their responsibilities sound.

The village chief does not stop resuming his advice. In case the leaders from the borders from where those individuals are originated did not view "The action of stealing to be a dreadful offense, well those individuals would have to hear it here. The chief would acknowledge that their repetitive announcement would sound boring to the people, but they would conclude that, it bears repeating in order to prevent any excuse of not being aware of Ambi Penalty which has no compassion.

And therefore we, the village chiefs estimate that it is crucial to educate everyone about a robbery offense and its consequences thereafter. It is necessary to explain thoroughly the reason why a theft had to undergo the "ambi ceremony" without pity!. It is not because the village rulers are rude or lack any degree of compassion. "*It is vitally important for all the constituents to become productive rather than exhibiting a lethargic, or envious and mischief attitude towards one another. . This is the bottom line why we sound redundant in this matter.* The chief would conclude his message.

Chapter III

DIVORCE CASE OF LARCENOUS VICTIMS

CASE No. III

Traditional marriage is a serious commitment, the groom's family work very hard to finalize the traditional wedding. The groom gets really scrutinized to prove his commitment to the bride. There are in fact many steps involved before both families could reach a final agreement concerning dowry. Certainly without an agreement, both the bride and groom can never be pronounced as "husband and wife." This is one of the reasons why, spouses do not get divorced easily in the Bantu/Congolese society. The cause of divorcing each other had to be evaluated seriously, prior to sealing the ultimate divorce step. The case should always be brought before the clan leaders first along with the family members, for a serious assessment. And subsequently, it would be brought to the traditional judges (Mbaku (uhm-baku), for hearing. When the reason for divorce is found to be legitimate, such as in the case of Ambi victims; since the case was already brought before the Mbaku (uhm-baku), the clan leaders, all the family members, and the witnesses; it was evaluated and also was found to be legitimate. And therefore, the wives of the larcenous victims have the right to divorce their husbands, if they choose to do so, the judges would proceed.

SETTLEMENT OF DOWRIES AFTER A DIVORCE

WHEN CAN THE MARRIAGE DOWRIES BE REIMBURSED IN CASE OF DIVORCE?

Basically, the marriage portion comes from the groom's family, and therefore, when the couple decides to go through a divorce, eventually the bride's family is responsible for reimbursing the dowry; that is, if the wife has been found guilty during the trial. However, based on the Congolese traditional law, if the husband has been found guilty of any offense, in that case, his wife' s family is not obligated of reimbursing anything to the husband's family; whether in terms of monetary or livestocks, which were offered prior to their wedding. The reimbursement of the dowry, generally occurs after the completion of the divorce procedure, which is known as, the washing of the hands and the running away activities which were previously discussed as the final and crucial steps of finalizing a divorce.

HOW DO THE WASHING OF HANDS AND THE RUNNING CEREMONIES ARE PERFORMED?

The Mfumu (uhn-fumu) judges and Mbaku (*uhm-baku*) lawyers) would provide a medium basin full of water, which will be placed before the audience. The court would also provide two stools facing each other, for the couple to be seated. The basin of water would be placed right between both stools and a soap bar.

Finally, Mfumu and Mbaku (uhm-baku) will seated facing the audience, then the moderator-judge would call the couple to step forward; and would again question both husband and his wife simultaneously, whether or not they had actually thought over any possibility of reconciliation? If both parties choose divorce instead of reconciliation, the judge then would order the plaintiff and the defendant to be seated on their respective little stools. The judge would speak the following words, "*Since none of the spouse has contested, we are now proceeding with the washing of the hands ceremony.*" The judge would hold the soap in his hand, and then, he would initially order the plaintiff to wash the defendant's hands.

The plaintiff would have to be the first to state the following words, while performing the washing of his or her partner's hands: "*Call the partner's name: example:* **Malata**, *"As of this day, I am setting you free! Please acknowledge that as of this day, you and I shall no longer be called husband and wife! I give you your freedom to marry another individual of your choice, without any hard feeling whatsoever!*" The partner involved, would reply, "*Yes, I acknowledge it, and I accept your divorce as of today.*" And then, the defendant would also wash the plaintiff's hands, stating, "(*the partner's name would be called first, example,* **Bakula**, *you too, as of this day, I am also setting you free before the Mbaku (uhm-baku), our respective families and all* *the witnesses gathered here. Further, please remember also that you and I are no longer known as husband and wife. I am therefore setting you free with no hard feeling, and you have the freedom to select any partner you choose to marry!"*

HOW DOESTHE RUNNING ACTIVITY OCCURS WHEN THE DIVORCE HAS BEEN PRONOUNCED?

After the washing of the hands ceremony, a moderator or a Mbaku (uhm-baku) would add, calling the couple by their first names, example: *Mutindu* (husband) and *Azola* (wife): We the Mfumu (uhm-fumu) (judges), the clan leaders and your respective families have all witnessed the confirmation of your divorce. *Bear in mind however that, "As of this Day, you are a divorced couple.* Each of you is set free in the eye of our **Nzambe** (uhn-Zambah)-**Mpungu** (uhm-Pungu) meaning our God, and in the eyes our ancestors, as well as all the people who are gathered here, presently. So, both of you now, should remember the following statement, *"Neither of you is required to demonstrate any slightest degree of jealousy on each other's future relationship."* Finally, the moderator would give the following order, *"And now to close the ceremony, the divorcees, (husband and his wife) would have to follow the directions given by the Judge presiding the divorce ceremony, which is the running away activity.* **How does it operate?**

The crucial step of sealing divorce judgment is actually to listen carefully and pay attention to the judge (Mfumu (uhm-fumu) or Mbaku (uhm-baku)'s order. The judge would have to first instruct the couple prior to giving them an order to perform the simultaneous running activity to the opposite direction. They are to start at the third count, *One, Two, and Three (at the third count,* he would then order the couple to *Now, GO and RUN!"* So, at this particular moment, both divorcees must run their heads off towards an opposite direction. However, as a rule, while they are running away from each other, they should not look backward, until they are disappeared from each other's sight, as well as that of the judges, the jury and the crowd gathered there, until they enter their respective homes.

Bear in mind that this is an ultimate step, which will make the divorce official. And therefore, should any individual look behind, even slightly, while performing the running activity, that person would be disqualified, should the judge perceives such a movement. *Why would it be so?* Because by law, this would indicate *violation against the traditional law*, which is regarded as a profound document; and as a result, that individual would have to pay a fine to the court of law. The Judges feel that they have to uphold the code of conduct rules.

THE TOUGH MAMA (Mrs. Kilakata) and Her

PETS' PUNISHMENT)

Can Pets Get Punished for Stealing around Their Owner's Home? Would It Be Considered As An Offence? Why? Who Had Developed Pets' Penalty?

There was a lady called Mama Kilakata in the village of Bandundu region, around Luniungu Sector in the Congo RDC. Due to her strong personalities she was called Mama Kilakata in Kikongo language which means a "Tough Mama". This lady invented a special punishment which was designed just for mischievous pets. For quite some times, the Tough Mama had been noticing that her Dog called (Bobete) and her Cat called (Kosito) were both becoming naughty. Apparently, they were acting unfairly to their owner who endeavored in taking good care of them. Mrs. Kilakata was devoted to her pets. They were very well fed, and she kept them very clean. Nevertheless, at the absence of their owner both pets would play dirty tricks on her. Eventually, she could no longer tolerate her pets' behaviors. Even though, at first, the Tough Mama had been very tolerant of her ill-behaved pets. However, pets would sneak behind her repeatedly, and would eat her son's favorite dish (Shrimps cooked in pumpkin seed), and sometimes they would eat the fish and meat left over in the kitchen, which could be served for the following meals.

Though, she would sometimes be a little upset with her pets, but no action would be taken against them. This situation was actually going on for quite sometimes, and she began getting irritated. Ultimately, she began noticing that both pets were overdoing their little tricks, which appeared quite annoying to the lady. Naturally, she started getting frustrated with her cat and dog's mannerism of eating up practically all the food (Shrimps, fish and meat) left behind. So, one day, Tough Mama was panic-stricken because her pets had ruined her plans. She had invited few guests for dinner at her home. And those guests were relatives of her very close friends who were visiting just for a week stay in her village. She was aware of their taste, so she had planned to cook a fish in order to offer her special guests on the following evening. Thus, she had left a big chunk of smoked fish on her stove that day.

When the Tough Mama had gone out to meet her daily obligations, unfortunately, behind the lady, Bobete (the dog) went in the Kitchen, sat down over the stove, and ate up everything. As soon as the owner had returned home, surprisingly, she apprehended Bobete (the dog), was getting ready to finishing up the remainder of that fish. Apparently, Bobete (the dog) was really enjoying the fish, noticing the manner in which it was jerking its head up and down, and passing its tongue around its mouth left and right, *reported the tough maman, angrily*!

The lady could hardly believe her eyes, suddenly, she exclaimed! ***"Bobete, how could you eat all this fish*?"** You were well fed, prior to my going out. How could you possibly eat all this fish? Swiftly, the dog (Bobete) jumped from the stove and ran out. The Tough Mama was left spellbound with her hands crossed over her head, murmuring, *"Bobete, I do not know what I can possibly do with you?"* Considering the fact that the guests were already invited, as an alternative, Tough Mama had to catch a chicken, and prepared it for her guests. She was eventually upset for such a sudden change from her initial plan.

She would have preferred to serve her guests a fish rather than chicken, although it did not matter to her guests. They had enjoyed eating that tasty chicken which was authentically cooked with all the exotic spices which emphasized its flavor. Even though it had been several occasions that Bobete (the dog) and Kosito (the cat) had eaten the leftover food, that particular time however, was crucial for the Tough Mama, because it had disrupted her initial plans. She was really furious with her dog, *she said.*

Based on that scenario, Mrs. Kilakata (Tough Maman) began wondering, "Why can't the rulers of her society design a special penalty for pets that would steal around their owners' homes similar to Ambi, which is attributed to the theft individuals? In fact, pets should be charged for stealing as well, because they are committing an offense, and why not? We have noticed that all the newly arrived individuals in our villages have learned the hard way. They thought, the village rulers would tolerate their unethical behaviors which they have acquired in their remote societies, apparently, they are now scared to steal in this society, because they do not wish to undergo the "Ambi Ceremony which has been designed for larcenous victims. The lady reported that pets should start getting punished as well, so they too could learn the hard way, and would be afraid to steal.

Bobete (dog), and Kosito (the cat) even though they are animals, they needed to be trained and be disciplined the hard way, through a special punishment which would scare them and prevent them from stealing behind their owners' backs. *Tough Maman reported angrily*.

Due to all those negative experiences which she had gone through with her cat and her dog, Mrs. Kilakata (*the Tough Mama*) was inspired to invent a simple, but effective punishment dedicated just for domestic animals. And therefore, she issued a warning to her pets, telling them that, "The next time you, my domestic animals, whether you Kosito (*the cat)* or you Bobete (*the dog*) would wind up acting badly, or stealing behind my back again, you would really get punished severely." She concluded that, "If stealing is bad enough for human beings, well, it should be regarded as being bad for the pets as well; because human beings and pets were created by the same *Creator* who requires order and decency. Further, the same *Creator* also desires to see everyone living happily, harmoniously, and joyfully in this planet Earth. The Creator demands that every creature exhibits a loving and peaceful behavior towards one another. Mrs. Kilakata also believed that showing discipline and a refinement demeanor would actually allow tolerance of each other. She also said, "I do not care whether it is dealing with human beings or with domestic animals, everyone should actually be living harmoniously with each other. All misconducts are bad either from human beings or from domestic animals.

Furthermore, everybody should pay all their debts as our traditions demand it. We should owe nobody. We must be the *providers* and the *lenders* and not another way around. Everyone is aware to pay his or her debt on time, without waiting to be asked. So why should animals around the house believe that they should take advantage of their owners? They would have to be disciplined in the same way that human beings are being shaped. *She reported, fuming.* And therefore, any creature, whether it is human beings or pets should be subject to some kind of punishment, once they act immorally to the point where they would upset the owner or somebody else.

It would actually be fair for every creature in the world to meets the law of restitution which does not discriminate, and which is inevitable. Let us all reap whatever we sow so that we could live fairly, *she asserted*.

Because Mrs. Kilakata (the Tough Mama) was so determined to punish her pets the next time any similar situations would actually occur. She maintained her promise of disciplining her pets, because the lady felt that she had had enough of those bad surprises. And therefore, they were subject to face a disciplinary action. So, a few weeks thereafter, she decided to purchase a big fish from the village Chief's fish pond. The fish raised in that pond had a very high reputation of having an exquisite taste, *reportedly*.

She therefore, decided to fry that fish in order to have it ready for diner with her family, on that particular evening. Based on her past awful experience with Bobete and Kosito, Mrs. Kilakata had taken some precautious measures prior to going out and meet her other obligations. She had completely ensured the protection of that fish.

So, after preparing the fish, the lady ensure to cover the frying pan with a heavy ceramic lid in order to prevent the dog or the cat from removing it, and be tempted to eat the food, as usual. Further, prior to leaving her home, Mrs. Kilakata made sure also to feed Kosito (the Cat) and Bobete (the dog) very well, as she had always done, *she stated*.

Mrs Kilakata and her Pets' Routine

FOLLOW STORY BELOW SEE WHAT HAPPENED TO

THE DOG AND THE CAT IN TERMS PENALTY

Which Pet would initially undergo the Tough Maman' Punishment?

Regardless to all of the precautions the Tough Mama had taken, shortly after her departure, Kosito (Cat) had made the first attempt to go into the kitchen, because it was attracted by the fish's aroma. Kosito sought every necessary means of uncovering the lid from the frying pan so that it could possibly eat the fish. Unfortunately, it met with a failure, because the lid was heavier than its entire body. In addition, that pot was hermetically closed, and Kosito (the cat) was unable to lift it out. As a result, Kosito had to leave it alone. Therefore, it departed from the kitchen. *A relative told Mrs. Kilakata that she had perceived her cat, turning around her kitchen that day for several times.* Subsequently, Bobete (the dog) suddenly, smelled the fish's aroma, and was immediately attracted towards the lady's kitchen, where the fish was located. Bobete was convinced that aroma was actually coming from that pot.

Unlike Kosito, Bobete (the dog) was able to push the lid away from the pan in order to expose the content. And thereafter, Bobete began to eat the fish, one piece after the next. Ultimately, it got to the last and the smallest piece. Right at that particular moment, Mrs. Kilakata (*KELAKATA*) had walked in, and apprehended Bobete seating comfortably; and it was attempting to finish up the last piece of that fish. The lady could hardly believe her eyes. She was dismayed to notice that the dog was able to remove that heavy lid away from the pan. So, she once again screamed! "Oh! Bobete! It is you again doing the same dirty trick on me? How can you possibly be so greedy when you were well fed prior to my going out?" *The Tough Mama exclaimed*!

The neighbor and the other family members, who were just returning from their daily activities had at first thought that Mrs. Kilakata (*KELAKATA*) was quarreling with another person, and yet she was addressing to Bobete (the dog), fiercely. The people heard Tough Mama yelling, "Bobete, this has actually been going on for quite some times, now? How can any human being put up with these badly behaved pets?" Well Bobete, she continued, this day would have to be the beginning of your **PILI-PILI** *(pele-pele)* PUNISHMENT!

The lady continued, "Remember dear Bobete, I actually sounded a warning to both of you, Kosito and you, Bobete; whether you heard me on that day or not, I am not concerned about your being pets, except that my promise will have to be fulfilled as of this day. I am conscious that you are a domestic animal, but due to the fact that you have been disobedient, I would like you to feel the heat today; so that in the future, you will stop misbehaving. I really have had it with your stealing action.

What a dismay having such pets like you and Kosito around my house! Generally, domestic pets are supposed to help individual to relax, but it has been an opposite with both of you. And therefore, my patience has actually run out; due to that reason, I cannot revise my initial decision of penalizing everyone who steals around this house. It does not matter whether you are human beings or pets, fish, flowers, or any living entity in this house; and that with no exception, would have to undergo either the Ambi paint or a Hot Pepper (pele-pele) punishment. We are talking about being fair to everyone and to everything," *Concluded Mrs. Kilakata, well known as the candid person.*

She actually became enraged with the action of her pets that she was determined to punish whichever pets that would aggravates her, especially from stealing. And therefore, in order to punish the dog, she took one big red pepper, and then, she cut it open from its head first.

Although Mrs. Kilakata (*KELAKATA*) was addressing her dog, obviously, Bobete had no idea what the lady really meant.

Shortly afterwards, she called the dog, "Bobete come here!" As soon as the dog approached her, the lady actually held it; and then, took the red pepper, and began to rub it around the dog's mouth. After the completion of her action, she dropped the dog on the floor; and ordered it, "Now, go away Bobete! I do not want to see you here around this house any longer, because you are full of wickedness!" The dog was seen staggering, and eventually it began feeling the heat from the reaction of that hot pepper. Finally, Bobete began to scratch the ground with its mouth; the pepper eventually was too hot around its mouth.

Shortly after that, the dog started barking while it was rubbing its mouth over the ground, from left to right; probably that was to seek some type of relief. The dog was actually pacing up and down. It felt helpless from the reaction of that hot pepper. Tough Mama began talking to the dog, saying, "That is your compensation of being naughty, Bobete! It is necessary that you learn your lesson today. She was making fun of Bobete, stating, "Go ahead Bobete, and rub that mouth so well on that ground. She continued, "Let that hot pepper bites you really good!" The dog was running from left to right, seeking some assistance which it could not find eventually. Mrs. Kilakata (*KELAKATA*) said to her dog, "At least Bobete, you have given me some satisfaction now that you are feeling the heat. This is just the application of the law of Nature or the law of restitution. Please believe me that I am not actually attempting to be abusive. It is you who have been abusing me all this time regardless of how good I treated you and Kosito, the outspoken lady, replied to everyone who was inquiring in regard to the approach she had taken. *In fact, her critics had mixed reactions.*

She continued talking to her dog, "You have been the one who'd been abusing me as well as my entire family, such as depriving my guests from having the meals that have been planned to serve our special guests or even my entire household. Further, you have been depriving my family and myself from enjoying our planned meals. So, get it now!

Evidently, you overdid it, and you have been causing me unnecessary tension and pressure! Well, the French people say, "*Rira bien, qui rira le dernier*" (**He who laughs last, laughs longest**)." After that incident, the family members noticed Bobete's disappearance from the house, for quite some time, because Mrs. Kilakata had repeatedly told it that, "I do not want to see you around my house again."

Obviously the dog sensed it and suddenly, ran away to Tough Mama in-laws' home, where it had also formed the habit of stopping by occasionally with its owner. Apparently, Bobete had developed a high degree of fear around Tough Mama. Her family noticed that every time the dog was passing around Tough Mama's house, it appeared so fearful, and was watching Tough Mama from afar, *said Tough Maman.*

Mrs. Kilakata, the Tough Mama Wondered, "How is it that the Mfumu (uhm-fumu) of her Society, or the Lawmakers of that time had completely failed to conceive any type of Penalty designed just for *Domestic Naughty Animals*, which could be equivalent to the "AMBI Paint" which was designed appropriately for *thieves*?

And therefore, she figured that since there was no such thing, "I would invent or create one serious punishment for pets. The lady argued that pets are creatures too like others. They enjoy people's company as much as people enjoy theirs, and therefore, they should be trained and punished to some degree, in their own special way. Because human beings have the "Ambi paint," pets should have something to scare them as well, and therefore the "*HOT PEPPER*," I believe, is quite a propos." Tough Mama continued to argue that her newly designed pets' penalty would prevent them from causing any type of chaos and irritation to their owners who are already busy with all other human daily responsibilities.

In fact with respect to her critics, the bold lady replied, "*I am quite certain that my action will continue to sound hilarious to many people, and rude to others, but any pet who wishes to live in association with me must act docile. However if the pet is not submissive it should be punished for its incompliance, or I would have to dismiss it, period!*

Since it is our ancestors' norms which require that everyone should live in such a peaceful environment, and therefore, when I come home from a strenuous labor, I would like to see docile pets around me. Those which are discordant have to remain away from me, from now on.

Mrs. Kilakata (*KELAKATA*) or the Tough Mama was somewhat illumined, suddenly, she remembered her great uncle statement regarding. He had said, "Criticism has always been in every society, it not possible to escape that element. However, besides from criticism, wise people may arise; and discover some truth out of that seeming unsuitable concept. Ultimately, from a strange idea, wise people can develop a constructive concept which other individuals can be benefited from, soon or later." The bold Mama stood for her idea, even though some individuals did deride it, but others adopted it. She was viewed as an intelligent Mfumu (uhm-fumu) Nkento or Woman Chief to many. Her pets' penalty was termed "Pili-Pili (pele-pele) or hot pepper."

Apparently Kosito would have been the first pet to undergo the Hot Pepper Punishment which the bold lady or Tough Mama had actually invented. However, its being frail to uncover the lid from the Pan at Tough Mama's stove, had actually saved Kosito from being the first to be penalized. Nevertheless, Kosito was not exempt from its swindling activities. It cheated as many times as the dog did.

Certainly, the cat has no slightest idea about Bobete's (*the dog*) suffering from that hot pepper. Bobete's barking actions did not mean anything to Kosito (*the cat*). Apparently, it did not meddle with Bobete's problem, it acted as innocent as it could appear.

Kosito was seated quietly in its little corner; and was trying to prove how obedient and innocent it has been to its owner. However, it did not take long for Kosito to realize that it was not excluded from the hot pepper punishment. Tough Mama had sounded the warning not only to Bobete (the dog), but to both of them. In reality, that warning was applicable to any pet she would ever own in the future; and specially the pet that would steal around her home. Tough Mama's decision had always prevailed, because she was known to her associates as having a strong personality, which was probably due to the fact that she was originated from the royal ancestors, where she had been instructed since childhood that in life you must learn how to address any issues fearlessly. Further she was instructed that she should not rationalize any issues in order to conceal the consequences involved. Additionally, she should learn how to reply to any questions frankly.

In fact, she became a clan leader after the death of her brother who was a family ruler during that time. Mrs. Kilakata was ultimately ordained as Mfumu (uhm-fumu) Nkento or a Female Chief) who became a very influential lady in her village, according to oral traditions.

Trial: "Deceitful Case

CASE No: IV"

The Cat (Kosito) and Mrs. Kilakata (theTough Mama)

It is not clear whether or not the Tough Mama acted spitefully when she actually left the cooked meat on the stove that day; covering the pot with a light lid. She thereafter, had gone out to conduct her usual business. Prior to leaving her house, the bold lady ensured feeding her pets adequately as usual. Kosito's episode occurred one month after Bobete's hot pepper initiation. Unfortunately, Kosito was ensnared, and as a result, it underwent the same treatment that Bobete did. By observation, Kosito exhibited almost the same signs of suffering as well as Bobete; such as rubbing its mouth on the ground, pacing-up and down and running around the property; and also, stopping every now and then and nuzzling the wall. That rubbing movement was to seek some alleviation from that hot pepper's reaction apparently. Gradually, the intensity of hot pepper subsided, *affirmed Tough Maman.*

However, shortly after that incident, things worked out differently. The lady said that one day, she had noticed three huntsmen from the country borders came by her village. They were seeking to buy few dogs which they desperately needed to train for their hunting activities. As soon as they had perceived Bobete, they were immediately attracted to it, because Bobete appeared beautiful and a healthy dog. Therefore, those people inquired about buying Bobete right then. So, Mrs. Kilakata was contacted right away. She was asked whether or not she would be interested to sell Bobete to those huntsmen. The Tough Mama replied to the huntsmen that, "You do not actually need to buy my dog. I am willing to offer you Bobete, free of charge.

It would be wonderful, if Bobete could get itself such an honorable hunting job, which would keep it very busy. Apparently over here Bobete appeared bored to death, she concluded." In fact, that situation was perceived to be such a perfect coincidence. It was a wonderful opportunity to get rid of Bobete, once for all, *reported Mrs. Kilakata.*

The huntsmen were grateful to Mrs. Kilakata (*KELAKATA*) for having offered them such a wonderful gift. They gladly took Bobete to their village, and then began to train it in hunting activities. A few months later, Mrs. Kilakata (*KELAKATA*) was informed that Bobete was such a remarkable dog. It has such a keen sense of apprehending an animal. It runs after it eagerly, and catches it in a timely manner. Mrs. Kelakata was eventually happy to hear such a good report about Bobete.

66

She began sharing that good news with her neighbors eagerly. Did you hear this; she would said, "My dog reportedly has a keen sense of spotting animals, and going right after them. Seemingly, Bobete is such an asset to their business activities." What a perfect coincidence, she asserted.

As far as Kosito (the Cat) was concerned, after having undergone the hot pepper chastisement, suddenly, it disappeared from the Tough Mama's home. And, no one had seemed to know its whereabouts. Few weeks later however, it re-appeared, suddenly on its own volition; and went directly to seat at its usual corner. Kosito's re-appearance was such a hilarious scenario to Mrs. Kalakata's family, and especially the fact that it remembered to occupy its usual corner. Apparently, it was perceived that Kosito too, had developed some degree of fear towards its owner. However, things turned out differently from its regular routine. One Saturday morning, a gentleman from the vicinity came by Mrs. Kilakata's home, and noticed Kosito lying gently at its regular corner. He felt in love with it. All of a sudden, that individual exclaimed, "This cat appears so healthy, strong and beautiful! And Tough Mama replied, it looks so, because it is well taken care of here.

Further, I clean it with a special authentic soap, and I had invented or designed a special authentic cream to apply on the bodies of all my pets. That is really the reason why people view all my pets attractive. The lady was wise, regardless to her pets' weaknesses, the bold lady did not bad-mouth Bobete and Kosito, and after all she loved them, regardless to their treacherous behaviors.

The gentleman continued, this is actually the type of a Cat that I really need to have in my home in order to help me catch the mice around my house. Mrs. Kilakata (*KELAKATA*) paid attention to that gentleman's statement; and verified it once more. The man spoke right away to Mrs. Kilakata, and said, "I am actually looking for a Cat to buy. I really need to buy it immediately. Would you know anyone who wishes to sell a cat?" The lady asked him, "Would you like to have my cat?" The gentleman replied, "Absolutely, I would buy it right now; how much can I offer you for this beautiful cat?" She replied, "Believe me if you need a cat that bad, you may actually have Kosito, right now! I will offer you free of charge." The man was somewhat shocked, and he was overwhelmed with joy, *reported the lady*.

As a matter of fact, we call her Kosito, *she explained*. Then, suddenly, the lady called Kosito to come towards her, and then, the cat obeyed, and immediately it approached the lady. She held that cat first, and handed it over to that man, and said to him, "Here, you may have Kosito today. It is yours now, but make sure to take good care of it and feed it well, because it is so accustomed to eating regularly. In fact, all our pets, they once belonged to our clan leader. They were always well taken care of since my family has never had a history of penury here, as you can see. Further, you must clean it or wash its body regularly, if you really wish to maintain its texture intact. Moreover, you should reserve a nice corner for its shelter. Additionally, Kosito adore a gentle touch, every now and then." The man was glad to have such a healthy and clean cat; so was Mrs. Kilakata (*KELAKATA*) for getting rid of her cat as well as her dog in such a harmonious way. Mrs. Kilakata (*KELAKATA*) was wise and reserved. She did not make any disparaging remarks about her pets. She actually freed them peacefully. *She reported to everyone who had inquired this situation.*

She reminded the people, our traditions are based on refinement manners, and therefore, in whatever we do, great parents had told us, we should do it using the wisdom of our ancestors. They said, "Living in this world, entails, we face various issues. People do not always act harmoniously. You will perceive diverse issues among the people, but you must learn how to resolve them, *using the intelligence that NZAMBI (uhn-Zambah)-MPUNGU (uhm-Pungu) had revealed our ancestors, only then that we can establish peace and justice in our society.* In fact, in the same manners I had dealt with my pets, it would be likewise with my fellowman. *We are not permitted to rationalize or conceal evil.*

Mfumu (uhm-fumu) Nkento (ehn- ken-to) (A Female Ruler/Chief)

In Bandundu region, gender plays a major role in terms of legal matters. Generally, the clan leader is supposed to be a male individual, based on social and cultural structure. However, it is permissible for a female individual to take over *the family's leadership, if the male entity does not exemplify the wisdom, the courage, and the strength expected to stand up before the village Chiefs/ Mbaku), in carrying out a debate in order to defend the interest of his family members, wisely.* A female African ruler is usually regarded as a powerful leader, based on her ability to defend and argue legal matters and touch the most important points which are overlooked by male leaders. During a trial, she has the power to raise her hand in order to interrupt and insert a statement which she estimates would lead to a correct, or to a fair decision. Apparently, she has naturally been empowered, and therefore, she must always be authorized to speak up. Usually, when she begins to speak, everyone is required to remain absolutely quiet; and analyze every single word which she pronounces.

Generally, male individuals or villages-chiefs are actually accustomed in acknowledging the wisdom of a female clan leader.

In effect, there is a saying in the Munsong tribe that states, "*ANY QUESTION* raised by a female ruler during a trial, should be honored immediately." It is so, because a female's brain is regarded as being a source of inspiration; which leads the trial to a fair verdict quickly most of the time. Generally, a female ruler is viewed as an individual who has a deep wisdom. She also has a decision-making skill to benefit the society. Further, she has a vision and ability to change situations swiftly and harmoniously. *This is the reason why, in the Bantu/Congolese society, a woman has always been addressed as, "Mama" which is a title of respect. Further the authority of a woman chief was always acknowledged by the court. It was not regarded as a threat to the male Mfumu (judges), because they knew that she was not exercising that power in any egotistical way. The woman recognized her duties as a wife and a mother. Therefore her ability was never smothered, until lately during our modern chaotic time.* Please read *"Africa presents the Congo RDC and Congolese Woman Chief (Mfumu-Nkento.)"*

Question: **What would happen to a Community, to a Society and to the WORLD, if every time that a mother would give birth, decides to destroy that child, thereafter? Where would you and I be today? And therefore, any nation that does not protect a woman or smother her progress is viewed as a DESTROYER OF THE WORLD.**

VIOLATION of Right

ISSUE

The Power of NFUMU NKENTO (A Female Ruler)

Mrs. Mayolo's family practiced matrilineal system. The political and social structure of her village was matriarchal. Therefore, her matriarchal uncle was known as an autocratic clan leader to some people due to his strength and firmness. In fact, when he was alive, nobody could ever attempt to take advantage of their family's property, as a rule, respect is regarded as a key word in the society. *Here is the situation*: At her family's property, stood a very huge tree which spread out an attractive shaded area on a sunny day. During the time that the uncle was living, no one else was allowed to sit under that tree, out of respect, except the family members and their guests, because it was a private property, and the tree stood right in front of their home.

Mrs' **Mayolo**'s village was located close to Luniungu Sector, she had two brothers. She was the youngest child. Her senior brother was enthroned a week prior the death of their maternal uncle who was their clan's leader. However, his leadership was viewed negatively. The brother could not exemplify any authority during any legal debate. In fact in Bandundu region, precisely by Luniungu Sector, *anyone who falls under this category is referred to as a person who lacks,* "**KIMBAKU** (kem-bah-ku). Mayolo had noticed suddenly, that the village chiefs began gathering and conducting judgment at that open attractive shaded area located right in front of Mrs. Kayolo's home without her being aware of such arrangement. Apparently, that was due to the fact that she was not the clan leader. Besides from that, she was a woman, additionally, on her family hierarchy, she was the youngest child. This concept in reality was out of the issue, as far as the traditions are concerned. She had been instructed from childhood that whatever belongs to a family member, it belongs also to the whole family, *according to the traditional law.*

From day one, Mayolo objected the idea of perceiving a crowd gathering right in front of her house. She repeatedly conferred this subject with her two brothers; and especially, the clan leader. However, her brother was unable to exert the qualifications of his leadership before the court. He appeared as though he was a coward, as far as the sister was concerned. As a result, all the village chiefs from vicinity, the jury, the witnesses, the claimant and the defendant families, concerned with the trial would all gather under that tree. They chose to do so, on a regular basis, without expressing any inconvenience. Eventually, it was quite disrupting to Mrs. Mayolo's privacy. She had decided to advise her village-chief, and complained repeatedly about that issue. And yet, she was totally ignored. This was actually an unusual perception, as far as the traditions' norms are concerned. Eventually, she could no longer handle such discord. She had had enough of watching these scenarios, and especially the fact that, her brother was unable to forbid the village officials to render that private property as a court house area. She knew that such practice was their cultural norms.

Mrs. Mayolo continued to whine, expressing her concerns regarding that gathering, which was being held in front of her home. But everyone, including the village chiefs ignored her again and again. They actually mocked her every request. And especially the fact that the bold uncle, whom was referred to sometimes as a LION was deceased and the new clan leader was just a frail man. All of them just rejoiced to gather under that beautiful tree in order to conduct their lengthy legal activities on a chosen Sunday afternoon. All the guests rejoice seating under that beautiful shaded area. Apparently, the guests had always assumed that it was being done with the family's accord, as the traditions require it.

Because Mrs. Mayolo was fed up with her village's chief's stubbornness, she was inspired to find a physical means of protesting against that unpleasant situation; and therefore, she conceived the way of chasing the crown once for all, from her family property, by disrupting the trial. Ultimately, after watering her vegetable in her backyard's garden, she was inspired to utilize the same technique the next time people would actually come, and gather under her beautiful tree in order to conduct their lengthy trial.

The lady had to apply her very simple, but high intelligence means, which nobody could have dreamt about. She had waited the Sunday which her village-chief had invited several other village-chiefs from the vicinity in order to assist in a very serious judgment. As usual, the crowd came in and gathered there with all the witnesses without any concern. They sat comfortably in front of Mrs. Mayolo's home, under that famous beautiful tree.

Mrs. Mayolo did not reprimand them on that day as she had always done, but rather, she waited until they got in the midst of a debate. She sneaked in her house, and went to prepare three big buckets full of water. They were placed right behind her main door. Obviously, she was ready for watering everyone seated in that crowd, the same way she watered her vegetable in her backyard. In fact her first target in mind was her village chief to whom she had addressed several concerns, and also reminded him repeatedly that his approach was ethically unacceptable; even though the village chief had been recently enthroned, he knew it. . He had received the traditional education like any other child since his childhood, so, he had no excuse whatsoever. Mayolo was just determined to act unethically as well. She had expected the aftermath of her action based on the Traditional Law. However she could careless at that time. She realized no such thing was ever done, while her bold clan leader was alive, therefore, she could not tolerate that view either. Mayolo made no selection among those people. She decided to spill water on everyone regardless to their social ranks, village-chiefs/Mbaku (uhm-baku) from her own village, or the dignitaries from the nearby villages, including the plaintiff and defendant and their respective families. She was fearless. She was just fuming, hearing all that persistent noise, which was going on in front of her house. Because the new chief acted immorally, Mrs. Mayolo was just ready to strike anyone that day; and did not care about any consequences which could result from her behavior. Based on her decision, she applied the French expression "*Que sera. sera*"- *Et qui vivra, vera.*" (Whatever will be – let it be and *whoever will live – will see*). She knew her action would be called a serious breach of conduct.

Mayolo waited until everyone's attention was placed on the debate, prior to beginning her watering activity. Unexpectedly, she came out with the first bucket of water. Initially, she abruptly poured almost three-quarter of the water over her village chief's head. Subsequently, she continued pouring some over the heads of every guest as fast as she could on other village-chiefs and other elite. After having depleted the first bucket, she quickly ran in the house in order to get the second bucket. She came out immediately, and she kept on sprinkling water over all the jury, or witnesses who had gathered there. While she was in the process of sprinkling water, Mayolo kept on addressing them the following words, "*ALL OF YOU NOW! GET OUT OF HERE! ALL OF YOU, OUT OF HERE, YOU GO*!"

Suddenly, everyone stood up simultaneously, and began departing from the lady's property. All the chiefs were soaked and wet, but the rest of the people were partially wet. They began running away from the tree, and in the meantime, the Host sounded very apologetic to his guests of honor. He continued shouting, "Come on out people, and let us get out of here. The lady is just crazy!

However, the lady sounded stern, and to their remarks, she began replying, "I *SWEAR, IT IS YOU WHO ARE CRAZY! I AM NOT CRAZY!*

YOU ARE THE ONES WHO ARE CRAZY! PLEASE, MAKE SURE THAT YOU DO NOT GATHER HERE ANYLONGER! PLEASE, RETURN TO YOUR RESPECTIVE HOMES, OR GO AND HOLD YOUR JUDGEMENT SOMEWHERE ELSE. NOW NOTICE, HOW YOU HAVE BEEN WATERED! IN THE SAME MANNER I DO WATER MY VEGETABLE IN THE GARDEN. I DECIDED TO WATER ALL OF YOU! ***YOU ARE DISLOYAL TO OUR TRADITIONS. BETRAYALS GO IN PEACE!.*** *AND LEARN TO ADVOCATE THE TRADITIONAL LAW, THOUROUGHLY. ALSO, TRY TO UPHOLD OUR ANCESTORS' CODE OF CONDUCT RULES, ESPECIALLY, THE NEWLY ENTHRONED CHIEFS NEED TO APPLY IT DAILY AND BECOME ADAMANT AND TRUTHFUL.*

IN ESSENCE, IT IS YOU, THE VILLAGE LEADERS WHO SHOULD EXEMPLIFY, RESPECT AND ENSURE PEACE AS OUR ANCESTORS HAD DONE! APPARENTLY, YOUR VISION IS GETTING DIM. YOU SEEM TO GO ASTRAY, BECAUSE YOU ARE DUPLICATING FOREIGN TRADITIONS BY IGNORING MY RIGHTS, WHICH IS OPPOSITE TO OUR TRADITIONS. THE NEW CHIEF IS A DISTROYER OF OUR SOCIETY WHEN HE IS SUPPOSED TO BE AN AVOCATE INSTEAD OF BEING AN OPPONENT OF OUR TRADITIONS. THIS IS WHY YOU ARE GETTING WHAT YOU DESERVE! ***SHE SHOUTED!***

Although, Mayolo sounded as though she had lost her mind, but in reality, she was in her sound mind. In fact, she meant every word she said. The lady spoke with confidence and audacity. She was fearless, because she knew, she was right, according to the oral traditions.

Mrs. Mayolo kept on repeating her message as she watched everyone running away from her property; shaking their wet clothes and hands. Some were wiping out water that was dripping from their faces.

In fact, most of the dignitaries were soaked and wet! They were eventually dismayed to go through such a degrading experience. Apparently, they had no slightest idea about what was going on between the host (the village head) and Mrs. Mayolo's issue.

Because of that situation, the trial was no longer held at that location. Most of the people had assumed that Mrs. Mayolo was somewhat crazy, but in reality, she was very bright or bold. She had to take this approach in order to stop that lack of consideration or respect, which was foreign to their traditions.

The lady was actually aware that that spirit of discord reflected the injustice, disrespect and negligence of the contemporary chiefs who appeared to believe that they were above the law, thereby attempting to duplicate the foreigners' cultures which the ancestors had actually rejected long ago. And yet, the true traditional law requires submission or obedience to ancestors' virtues. The wise lady concluded that such confusions were originated from the impostors who had been entering in the land illegally thereby finding ways to usurp our power and attempting in any means necessary to impose us their immorality, so that we could shy away to protect our values and let them stigmatize them as they had always done, but I could not hedge to disclose their intends.

Chapter IV

VIOLATION OF RIGHT

CASE No. VII

Tradition Law condemns violation of human right and inappropriate behavior in the society. Therefore, because of her inappropriate behavior at the village court of law, Mrs. Mayolo and her entire family was summoned to the court. Her action was regarded as a very big offense; and therefore, she had to be judged, severely. Her family had to answer to the court. They had to explain the reason why they had let Mayolo to disrupt the court session, by spilling water on the heads of the elite, the MFUMU and the Mbaku! Mayolo's clan leader and family were scare to death. They began reprimanding Mayolo since the first day she had committed that offense. It was already known that the outcome would actually be a severe penalty to the entire family for her misconduct. Mayolo acted inappropriately before the Mfumu (uhm-fumu) (village-chiefs) and their guests. Since Mayolo's senior brother who was the clan leader exhibited a passive behavior, he was frightened to appear before the judges due to his sister's behaviors.

On the day of Mayolo's trial, which was held at a different open area, Mrs. Mayolo was questioned, "

Question: Mfumu (Judge) – Would you explain the reason why you disrupted the court session?

Answer:- Mayolo I did it because our recently enthroned village chief broke our ancestors' law.

Question: Explain what law did your village chief break?

Answer: Mayolo: He violated the law of respect – Our traditions state, "Respect is our key word" – We all had learned that since our childhood. And I am aware that any issues should initially be addressed by a family's clan leader, but I took the stand to address it to my village chief since my brother was unable to do it. He had unfortunately ignored me.

Question: Mfumu – *Would you explain carefully what exactly have you requested, and why the village chief had denied it?*

Mayolo: *Since I was born, and since my uncle was the clan leader, I had never noticed a trial being held under the tree located right in front of my door. So I had requested such thing to be discontinued, and return the trial to its original location, but the village chief refused to do so.*

Question: Mfumu – *Mayolo do you know that you have actually broken the law for taking the place of your clan leader to address any issue regarding your family to the village chief?*

Answer: *Yes, I do, but my brother as you know is not capable to do it.*

He probably is under the impression that my deceased uncle would resurrect, and would continue to speak on the behalf of the family. I wish you to understand that by me taking the stand to address the family issue to the village chief, it does not necessarily mean that I intend to usurp the power, which was delegated to my brother. I know he had been enthroned. However I sincerely believe in our traditions. We all were taught to respect everyone and not to touch anything that does not belong to you since that would entail stealing. We also were instructed not to violate anyone else's privacy or right; because that would also be acting against the **NSIKU YA BA MBUTA** (breaking our ancestors' law).

Question: *Why then did you decide to begin pouring the bucket of water upon the Mfumu, the Mbaku, and the elite's heads first, instead of beginning with the common people?*

Answer – Mayolo - The lady was bold, smart and wise to begin with, and she replied, "*I did it intentionally, because the village chiefs are public servants. Further, they are the dignitaries who advocate laws and decency in our society. In addition, they are the ones who demand villagers to maintain peace and respect among themselves. And therefore, I would assume that they would know better than to ignore my rights. I reiterated the fact that this tree was never designated to become an official place to hold the judgment, but I was ignored.*

That is a legitimate reason. I had notified my village chief that the sight of the crowd and the persistent noise were quite disturbing to me and to my family. *Our ancestors never used to intrude or allow anyone to violate the privacy of their fellow beings.* I do not see why it should be allowed now? Amazingly, my requests have been ignored completely, under the guise of not being a clan leader. This is absolutely wrong, based on our *Bantu traditions; everyone knows that whatever belongs to one family member belongs to everyone within that family.* My being a woman or the youngest in the family is out of that question.

This fact just proves that you, the public figures, have actually ignored your own authority. Further, you have dishonored our ancestors' wisdom. Additionally, you have been taking advantage of my clan leader, because he is a passive man. I can remind you one fact though, when my uncle was alive, all of you used to call him an autocratic clan leader; if so, he was only exercising his authority in order to protect the interests of his family. He had no history of harming anyone or acting against our traditional law. He brought any issues to the court or to the Sector in order to obtain a fair verdict. My uncle did not believe in usurpation of anyone's power. Why hadn't you gathered here then during all that time that he was still alive? And yet, this tree had been standing here spreading out its shaded area for decades.

Because my uncle was bold, nobody conducted trials on my family's property, and yet this Tree has been standing here for years!

Question" Mfumu (Judge) – Mayolo, again do you remember that based on *our culture, the power to communicate with MFUMU (UHM-FUMU) (chiefs) during the trial is only given to the clan leader. So again how is it that you as a woman, who had not yet been ordained as a clan leader, could have the audacity of disrupting the court session?"*

Answer: Mayolo - "As you know the tree stands on my family's property. The property does not belong to my clan leader alone. True, it is actually a clan chief's duty to communicate with the village chief. He did not raise the issue, neither did my second brother. Considering the fact that all three of us did receive our cultural education from our parents since our early years, why shouldn't I speak up when my right is at stake, and the clan leader is frightened to bring forth the issue?

However, being that my brother's leadership is poor; our culture also states that a passive leader can be replaced by a bright family member, in order to guide the rest of the family as well as to protect the family's interests. Isn't that correct? I know if my brother had been a strong clan leader, and if he had been able to exemplify some degree of authority like my uncle did, he would have actually acted likewise. But, because he just isn't capable, and the second brother is a coward as well, then my being woman cannot prevent me from speaking up and protect what my ancestors had left me. This is not the usurpation of power, at all. I am quite sure that all of you standing here know that truth very well. I, like anyone else standing here, know the chronological history of my family, and nobody can actually fool me, even after the passing away of my so call autocratic uncle. I have acquired enough knowledge to be able to assume my family's responsibilities without failing my ancestors. *This lady was known as an outspoken individual. She knew how to capture her audience, according to the oral traditions.*

After, the judgment of Mrs. Mayolo, the Mfumu (uhm-fumu) decided that Mrs. Mayolo was actually a powerful woman, she had convinced everyone that attended the trial. *Therefore, the degree of her penalty was reduced to ONE GOAT and THREE CONTAINERS OF PALM WINE, instead of being charged triple.* However, since the Traditional Law is based on integrity, Nzambe/Nzambi-Mpungu/Mungu (meaning God the Great Being is actually presiding the Court, therefore the verdict must be given fairly. For this reason, all the Mfumu conferred and decided that *Mrs. Mayolo's* **village chief**, *had also to admit his mistake before God and before our ancestors. So, he too, was fined two containers of PALM WINE for having violated his constituent's privacy.*

The village chief acknowledged his weakness before the Court of law, and, especially before God and his ancestors who had entrusted him with that authority. As public servants they were actually supposed to give good examples, but they had failed to do so.

In fact, all the Mfumu together accepted therefore that *in the eye of their Nzambi-Mpungu (God the Almighty) and their ancestors, they were indeed wrong – Usually, in recognition of their human frailties, all the judges and lawyers who had conducted the trial had to chant* in unison, the acceptance of their errors, stating, 'Let our Nzambi-Mpungu, be the Winner of this complex *trial; and let us, the frail human beings admit our failure, before the Almighty as well as before our ancestors."*

Prior to sealing the trial, all the MFUMU – AND THE MBAKU – *should open that wine - and prior to drinking, everyone would have to take just a sip and pour some on the floor –they would remain few minutes in silence– in acknowledgement of their ancestors who had entrusted them with that wisdom, fairness, respect, integrity, peace, and justice.*

Ultimately, Mayolo who was at first criticized for her audacity, her family ordained her as a clan leader due to her ability to explain situations clearly, fearlessly, and in a convincing manner. She was known as the most skillful and wise clan leader, who is referred to as a Mfumu (uhm-fumu) Nkento (meaning a Female Ruler) in the Bantu/Congolese culture. Since she was ordained, she was empowered to raise her hand during the trial and also be permitted to intervene; by asking any relevant questions pertaining to that case. As a Mfumu-Nkento (Woman chief), she had acquired the authority to stand up, and speak on the behalf of her family's matters appropriately and make any intelligent declarations.

Whenever she stood up to intervene in any misleading judgment, everyone had to remain silence, and listen to her talk without any interruption. She was actually viewed as a gifted woman chief. Based on her decision-making skills, the lady was extremely capable of guiding the rest of the judges in terms of deciding any case; even the most complex cases in a fairly manners, *according to our oral traditions.*

VIOLENCE CASE:"Mr. EDONKE & COUSIN MUSANGA"

CASE N0: VI

THE TRADITIONAL LAW PROHIBITS THE SHEDDING OF BLOOD

In the Bantu/Congolese society, and especially in Bandundu region, precisely in Luniungu Sector, the traditional law prohibits any slightest incident that would cause the shedding of another human being's blood. It does not matter whether the incident has occurred accidentally or intentionally. Any shedding of the blood, whether it appears insignificant or a big cut would still be regarded as an act of violence against another part of life; and therefore, it would require a serious judgment in the Congolese traditional courts of law. As a result, the individual who has caused such an incident would have to be charged with a fine corresponding to the degree of that cut, as well as to whatever motive that laid behind that incident.

Shedding of Human Blood (Violence)
VIOLENCE CASE
Trial Case No. VI

Mr. Edonke, Lwambe was born in a remote part of the Congo RDC. His grandfather was a descendant of an ancient Greek, a merchant who had chosen to be settled in the Democratic Republic of the Congo, after having experienced several years of harmonious associations with the natives of Congo. The Greek merchant actually refused to return to his native country, regardless to the numerous invitations received from his folks. His folks erroneously believed that the Congolese people were vicious or ferocious to foreigners. The Greek man, who had actually had a personal experience dealing with the people of Congo, denied their allegations. He also ignored his family's consecutive invitations; he was always mocking the content of their correspondence and used to translate it to his wife and children.

He was writing back, and ensuring his folks that such a claim was actually false, according to his own personal experience dealing with the Congolese people. As far as the man was concerned, he would write back to his family and friends that, *"Truly, the natives of Congo were on the contrary, very courteous, friendly, loving and very spiritual. The only time that the people would use their **BIPUPU (MACHETTES)**,* Tolo-Tolo, *BIKASI - Special Arrows, or* *any other sharp devices, and Lance, would actually be, just for self-defense against those who cunningly seek to harm them. Who wouldn't act likewise, in Grece or anywhere else on this Earth? Seeking protection is just a human nature which no individual can deny it. That is quite, natural, I believe, he would conclude.*

The foreign merchant would further explain to his folks, the circumstance under which the people would rebel violently, and decide to utilize their means of protection, just for self defense. "Since I have been in association with the Congolese natives, I had noticed that the pagans do utilize their ancestors' mysticism to riposte against those deceitful outsiders who are always seeking to meddle with their properties or looting their ancestors' resources. However, it ought to be a serious motive underneath it. People in general live in a non-violence society. Further, while the pagans act according to their belief, in order to find justifications against those evil people who attempt to approach their society with the wrong motives, staunch Christians however, call to their Nzambi-Mpungu (God, The Almighty), in order to seek His righteousness against the wickedness.

The Greek man would also write about how amazed he was to notice, the Congolese natives' spiritual illumination. Their Christian's belief and especially their fear of God, The Almighty, which they termed, Nzambi-Mpungu) was stunning. And yet, we were told that these people knew nothing about the true God except the worship of their little gods. That actually is untrue.

Having acquired sufficient knowledge regarding this society, the man learned local language and subsequently, he decided to change his Greek name to an African name. He became Edonke, Malandu. He then decided to marry a native woman. His first approach however, was not received easily to the lady's family. They were very reluctant at first, because they had thought he probably was one of the secret kidnappers, like many others, who pretend to act friendly, thereby offering some incentive to some natives, in order to seek ways to gain control and cause unnecessary destruction. At first, I was being watched closely.

He continued, truly, these people had been hurt for decades by our own people; and had developed a cynical attitude in order to convince my fiancé's family regarding my sincere desire to marry their daughter, was very tough indeed. I knew that my desire was genuine, and I sat with her clan leader constantly in trying to convince him. Seeing my sincere desire, finally, he had to explain to me all the necessary steps involved in marrying one of their family members, officially. This procedure is based on the ancient's wisdom, which was utilized to scrutinize a groom, in order words, to find out whether or not the desire to marry that woman was actually genuine. The Greek man confirmed also that he was willing to satisfy all the necessary requirements, based on the wife's culture. "

He continued, "Because everyone in my wife's family was convinced that my motive was truthful and that I had humbly showed a high degree of respect to their culture; due to that reason, my dowries were then honored. However, I had to ensure that whether my offspring or my wife would never be kidnapped by me or by any other merchants secretly or otherwise. Having proven my point, I was allowed to marry the lady. *The man related his narrative to his friends first, and then, later on, to his own children, who used to rejoice exceedingly to hear their father's experience in the foreign land.* He also recognized that he had actually been happily married to a staunch Christian woman, who had helped him to grow spiritually, *according to the oral traditions.*

Both, husband and his wife helped their twelve children to grow spiritually as well. Their children also had developed fear of "Nzambi-Mpungu" (God the Almighty) in their daily activities and respect to their ancestors' virtues. Further, the Greek man alluded to the *oral traditions session, which used to occur between grandparents and their grandchildren, whenever he wrote to his folks.* He wrote also how he had to observe and witness, the manner in which his mother-in-law used to gather his twelve children around her in order to reveal to them all the steps involved in their cultural education. She would begin from the origin of their maternal family. She would also inform the children, the really name of their tribe, as well as those of their great great grandparents, including the location where they had first been settled.

Moreover, she would also indicate the events, which had caused them to migrate from the previous areas to their current place. In addition, the mother-in-law would give all the necessary details in regard to everything which belong to the family such as the land, and also the manner in which their properties had been inherited.

The man confessed that he had nothing worthwhile to relate to his children except his past and poor mercantile experience, in Greece, which had forced him to seek a better life to Africa. However, he whispered to his children that on their father's side, they would be referred to as "Les Chypriotes" and that he was of the Orthodox faith and that in his country, his church was full of icons, which was very different from their church in that local area.

The mother-in-law would also explain to the children, how the village chief of that time, used to instruct them to run away against the Mundel-A-Bangombe (western kidnapers), *pronounce as* (**Mun-da-la bahn-gom-bah**). In fact, the chief used to advise its constituents, "God gave you children; So, remember, you must take good care of them. Further, if we suspect MaKieme (***Ma-ke a m a***) or foreign invasions, "Women must ensure to carry babies under their chests. Carefully, you as a mother must tie your Liputa (**leputah**) (*a yard of a fabric*) by the neck, and lay your baby in that pocket, a space created by that "Liputa" (**piece of material**). Make sure to secure it tied, so that you do not drop the infant while you are actually running away from the kidnappers.

In addition, if you have another child, you should tie the toddler on your back, secure the child well. Further, if you have two other children, the husband must hold them; one from each hand, while running away. The husband should make sure to grab some food to feed the children while running in the forest. If the man is caught by the kidnappers, the mother must continue running in the trails with the children. If the children begin to cry for food, stop in that area; and see whatever fruit you can collect to feed your children and yourself, but keeping on running until you reach at a safe place where you can settle safely, and preferably by the water, water fountain or a brook. Rest under the beautiful trees, Nzambi-Mpungu by His mysterious way had created some trees tied together in the form of Dome. So, should you find such an area, you may rest for few days; then, take the courage, continue to go further.

The village chief would insist that whatever you do, please, make sure that you do not drop the baby or leave your child behind in order to seek your own protection! This would actually be a crime against our culture, and especially, against our God, the Nzambi-Mpungu). Remember, the chief would make an inference, "Failure to save the children would actually result to a **Curse,** for lacking enough love to protect your children!"

Ultimately, the chief would remind the people, "Do not forget to keep on calling on Nzambi-Mpungu (our God Almighty) as you are running away. Tell God as you cry to him. We have not done any wrong to the kidnappers. This world belongs to you. You gave us this land and yet we are persecuted for no apparent reasons. We recommend all our enemies in your hands. The chief would add, "My people also do not forget to call upon our ancestors, so that they can enfold all our enemies, including their offspring in their spirit of everlasting *Curse,* because of their mischief, let them pay back to the law of nature!"

The Greek man would find the oral transmission of Traditional Law, from grandma to his grandchildren very fascinating indeed! He would actually confess to his Congolese wife as well as to his twelve children, *how different their cultures actually were from each other.* He would also show, and translate to his wife and to his children all his correspondence which he was addressing to his folks back home.

The man would also read and translate the correspondence received from his family, to his wife and children, begging him to return back home; even though the standard of living had remained in a status quo since he had left to begin his merchant's activities abroad. He would write back to ensure his folks that he actually was better off in the Congo than he had been home in terms of doing business with his newly acquired family. The Greek man would mock his brother's misconception, attempting to persuade him to go back to Greece and resume their previous little business activities. His wife and his twelve children would comment and all of them would make jokes at it.

The Greek man adapted local customs, because he did not want to be taken for a kidnapper like the other foreigners who appeared suspicious, and among them, some had been expelled from the country due to their wrong motives. However, he was such an open minded individual. He humbly learned practically how to do everything that his wife's family did without any reservation such as going to the forest to cut logs as well as fishing or catching fish from the family's fish ponds. He enjoyed eating Pondu dish with its exquisite aroma, and therefore he learned how to collect "Pondu vegetable (cassava leaves)" from the field and assisted his wife in cooking it, *according to oral traditions.*

The man was also involved in helping out with farming activities, such as planting palm trees and collecting palm fruit, bananas, and plantains. Furthermore, he continued conducting trading in the nearby towns with his brothers-in-law and some of his bigger sons.

Mr. Edonke's family, on his matriarchal side, lived in the home State which was adjacent to a very big village. The gentleman stood six feet tall, and was medium built. Unfortunately, Edonke had a stammering speech. Edonke and his distant cousin had always been in a very close association. They had developed a habit of travelling to the village in order to conduct some business activities on a regular basis. Unfortunately, there was only one bike which belonged to Edonke. Musanga had the habit of borrowing the bike whenever Edonke was not using it. One day however, Musanga had brought back the bike with a flat tire, and then he was gone without noticing Edonke of that particular problem. On the following day, Edonke needed to use the bike, however, he had realized that the bike needed a new tire which was not available at that time. Eventually, Edonke was somewhat upset, but not to the point of harming anyone. He then began amending the said tire, because he was about to utilize it. Suddenly, Musanga came up behind him; and when he attempted to touch him by his right shoulder in order to relate some information to him, at that particular moment, Edonke was in a bended position; and accidentally, he pushed Musanga away with his right hand.

Musanga, stumbled suddenly, and then, felt over a tiny piece of metal which was lying close by. As a result, he was wounded. Noticing the blood, Edonke dropped the bike immediately, and ran to assist him. Some of his family members had witnessed the incident, and came at once to assist him as well; and then applied a special traditional medicine on the wound. Shortly afterwards, the bleeding stopped. The incident was quickly reported to Musanga's clan leader, who in turn seized the village-chief in order to satisfy the culture's requirement, based on the traditional law. Shortly after that time, Edonke's trial was scheduled in two weeks.

Apparently, Edonke was terribly affected morally and physically since the day the incident occurred until the trial date. His wife was morally disturbed as well due to the fact that her husband had lost his appetite and enthusiasm. Eventually, he was afraid for the upcoming trial, because he anticipated the consequences of the blood shedding case.

Blood Shedding Trial
CASE No. VIII

On the day of the judgment however, while everyone including all the panel of judges arrived on time at the local court area, Edonke, who was the defendant, was missing. Obviously, he was frightened; because that was his first appearance in court. He knew he was going to stand before the judges who would pepper him with questions. Due to the fact that he was stammering, Edonke decided to drink more than enough water that day. Probably, he thought that having enough liquid in his system would calm him down, and would also permit him to speak fluently and calmly without stammering. He took this approach in the attempt to convince the jury that he had not pushed Musanga intentionally, but it happened accidently.

After an hour waiting for Edonke to appear in Court, the client was still at home, trying to figure out how in the world he would be able to convince the judges? Noticing that lengthy delay, his relative had to run in order to escort him to the court location. When he returned to get him, he noticed that Edonke was knelt down. He was uttering a little prayer. He was told that everyone was already present at the court awaiting him. Shortly after that, the messenger and Edonke came almost running to the court. As soon as he had arrived, he appeared breathless, and fearful due to the anxiety. The first thing that Edonke did when he was called to speak before the Mfumu and Mbaku (judges and lawyers) was to begin with a salutation. Edonke bowed at first in order to salute the panel of judges, prior to beginning saying a very first word, he began stammering, "*Ah..Ah..Ah..board of of judges, "Good afternoon*!" Everyone replied, "Good afternoon, Edonke!" Suddenly, one of the judges stated with a deep and authoritative voice yes good afternoon Edonke after having us waited so long to begin the trial. So he began:

Mfumu (judge)- "*As you know Edonke, everyone is gathered here to hear you explain to all of us, the reason why you have violated our ancestor's law of hurting your fellowman!*"

After hearing this statement, Edonke bowed again prior to beginning his narrative, and then, he saluted the panel of judges once more, struggling to pronounce the first word.

Answer - Edonke - "*Ah..Ah..Ah..board of judges, good afternoon!*" *They once again replied, "Good afternoon Edonke!"*

He stammered all along in the attempt to say his first word, *"As.a..as..a.. as..a matter of fact, Mu..mu, Musanga and, and, and, I, are, are a…..are not enemies, be..be..becau, bebe…cause.* Edonke, was actually sweating as he sought an appropriate word; he was kicking his right foot on the ground as he attempted to find a word to express himself.

Additionally, he was tapping his right hand over his right thigh. Suddenly, he requested a permission to stop for a while, so that he could quickly go to the rest-room. *He pleaded anxiously, "I had drunk plenty of water prior to appearing to this court, it is an urgent need"*, he said. He was then allowed to go quickly. And then, as soon as he re-appeared before the judges, again, he saluted the panel of judges, once more, **Answer -Edonke:** *"Ah…..h..Ah… board of judges, good afternoon!"* *Again they answered him, "Good afternoon Edonke!"*

The gentleman continued to stammer as usual, and still the words could hardly come out of his mouth. He also continued to kick his right foot to the ground, and tapping his right hand simultaneously over his right thigh. Sadly, he was struggling to pronounce a word, which was not audible at every attempt. The male chiefs started to become very impatient with Edonke. One of them stood up, and spoke harshly, **Mfumu (Judge)** - said: *"We just hope that you are not acting spitefully! Try to speed up because we are not going to lengthen the trial session* *just for your game. See, if you can try to be a little more cooperative with the court regulations. We urge you to stop being anarchist before the judges; if you actually wish to have a fair trial. In addition, do not forget that Musanga bled because of your violence; and all that the court needs to know is whether the incident happened intentionally or accidentally?"* Shorty after that question, another male judge stood up and added.

Question Mfumu (Judge) - *Mr. Edonke, our patience is running out! Would you hurry up, and stop kicking that foot on the ground, and tapping that poor thigh, it is very distractive to everyone watching you here. Certainly you do not want to be charged a double portion fine, and also be granted less time to gather the fine requested. So, try not to delay the session.*

Fortunately, the panel of judges was composed of four male judges and two Mfumu (uhm-fumu) Nkento (two female chiefs – usually clan chiefs in this case), among them were Mrs. Mayolo and Mrs. Kilakata. After hearing those harsh statements, they stared at each other for a few minutes, because they actually had realized that those male judges sounded cruel. Finally, Mrs. Mayolo raised her hand to request a permission to speak, as the norms require. She was granted the permission to stand up. *Hear female chiefs' intervention:*

Mfumu-Nkento (female chief) - *This individual is not actually trying to waste anyone's time. He just has a lot on his plate to handle; as you can perceive. Evidently, there are several elements which are hindering his speech.* **First of all***, the client has been known to everyone that he was born a stutter, and his speech impediment is out of his control.* **Secondly***, he had never appeared in court of law before, since he was born. These are actually things which we all should bear in mind as we proceed. Then,* **Mfumu-Nkento (female chief) Kilakata,** *added,"***The third thing** *is the fact that this man is experiencing an anxiety since he is unable to express himself accordingly. And* therefore, everything combined together is creating a chaos in his speech. The defendant does actually have a point to make, however he is struggling under an intense anxiety plus his disability. In addition, *the more he is trying to express himself, the harder it is getting for him to make any sense. So, let us be understanding, and let us realize that Mr. Edonke has an infirmity which is actually uncontrollable. And therefore, we female judges would like to make a request in regard to this situation. Our request is to be compassionate and considerate. It would be preferable that we do settle this case today without adjourning it at a later session. We really see no need to do that; since the consequences of bloodshed case has already been underlined by our traditions. I perceive no apparent reason to lengthen the trial. Let us preserve our fellowman.*

It would be preferable that we settle this client's case today so that we can free from stress and unnecessary pressure. Above all, let us realize that we are dealing with a human being, and not with an animal. **Mfumu-Nkento (female chief). Mayolo concluded that***: "Nevertheless, we are dealing with a blood shedding case, and the law requires a penalty pertaining to this case, one way or the other, so why can't we just decide the penalty, and free our fellowman who is already suffering, physically, mentally and morally? The claimant stated that Edonke did not actually do it in purpose, but it happened by accident.*

Having heard women's intervention, everyone agreed that indeed, the Mfumu (uhm-fumu) Nkento both sounded very reasonable. And from that point, the board of judges conferred and ultimately, the defendant was fined without any further discussion or questions. So, the case was closed, shortly after that discussion. According to the court's decision, **the verdict had been given as follow:**

Edonke, lost the blood shedding Case. His penalty was to pay three goats and three big bottles of palm wine. He was given one month to actually pay his fine to the court of law. According to the Bantu/Congolese culture, the entire family would have to chip to gather every items required by the Court, in a timely manners. From the court standpoint, however, all the judges would take the responsibilities in distributing that fine among the jurors and the client who had won the trial. They would determine what portion of that fine should be given to the claimant's family, and also which portion would be assigned to the Court according to the traditions.

Based on the Bantu/Congolese culture, when one family member gets in trouble, the burden falls on every family member, as we have previously indicated. And therefore, everyone must exercise a cooperative action in order to buy the three goats and the three big bottles of traditional wine needed to meet the court's obligation. This actually is the main reason why a clan leader is required to oversee the activities of every family member in order to prevent problems which would result unnecessary expenses to the entire family. *This is also a vital reason why any family member that keeps on bringing incessant issues in the family, was to be sometimes dismissed from the family. According to the oral traditions.*

Chapter V

A BREACH OF CONTRACT CASE

CASE NO. IX

A Tailor and His Client

Talent is known as a natural gift. Even in the remote part of the countries, or in the villages, one could find a gifted or a talented individual. Mr. Taweki was known to be the most talented Tailor in his village located in Bandundu region, precisely in Luniungu Sector. He could be comparable to some eminent designers in the western world, in terms of his ability to create style and make men's clothing meticulously. However, his fees could never equal to those other eminent world designers. He used to charge his customers a fee which was proportionately to the villagers' standard of living, so to speak.

Mr. Kasongo came from a well to do family. He always wore expensive material clothing which only the elite of his society would actually wear. One day, he decided to have a pair of trousers made by the Tailor, Mr. Taweki. The customer intended to wear that pair of pants on the upcoming friend's wedding.

The contract between the Tailor and his client was that the work should be completed within two weeks. The tailor had told the client to return by that time on a specific day, in order to pick up his pair of pants, and also to pay him his fees for his service.

However, the client, Mr. Kasongo happened to be around the Tailor area, a day prior to his scheduled day. And therefore, he just decided to stop by in case the work had been completed, and so, he could just pick up his pants, and pay his fees. Mr. Kasongo was well aware that he may have to come back, eventually, should the Tailor request additional time to finalize the work. But, he figured let me just take a chance.

Upon arrival at the Tailor's shop, Mr. Kasongo was shocked to notice that the Tailor had completed making his pants since a week ago, and he had been WEARING it all that time. Reportedly, the reason he wore it was out of curiosity to feel the touch of that elite fabric in the body. Apparently the type of that fabric was only worn by notable of the society. By wearing it those few days, the tailor wanted to feel as one of the elites.

Because the client had arrived unexpectedly, the tailor on the other hand, has the client's paints on his physical body; eventually, he had no valid excuse before the client.

The client perceived that the job was actually well done, and the tailor appeared gorgeous in that pair of pants. However, he was fuming to see such degradation. What *could the tailor really say under such circumstance?* He was just embarrassed. Words failed him to express himself.

The client was obviously furious, and he exclaimed, Taweki, I know this is the fabric I gave you to make me a pair of pants. When did you ever complete making this pair of paints which you are wearing? This was not our agreement. How is it that you are wearing my pants? He screamed! "Mr. Taweki, how is it that you are wearing my pants? **Take it off immediately!**" The tailor could hardly find any appropriate word to say to his client. The only thing he did under such circumstance was nothing, **but giggled all the way through just to hide his guilt.**

Taweki kept on saying a repetitious sentence such as, "**Oh, pal you were supposed to come here tomorrow, and not today**." He repeatedly said to his client, "our appointment was actually tomorrow, and not today. The tailor made Mr. Kasongo infuriated. *The client commanded the tailor, once more to take off the pants or else! He finally held him by the waist, and then the tailor finally took the paints off, still **giggling!***

THE TRIAL ON THE" BREACH OF CONTRACT CASE"

The Tailor and His Client

CASE NO. X

THE CASE WAS BROUGHT TO THE COURT

Mr. Taweki, the tailor and Mr. Kasongo the customer were scheduled to appear in court on a set date.

Question – Mfumu (Judge) The tailor was called and asked, *"Did you and the client make an agreement that you will have to wear the client's pants after the completion of your work?"*

Answer- The tailor, *facing the floor, "Well, actually no."*

Question - Mfumu (Judge) *-The tailor when did you complete the work?"*

Answer (Tailor)-, *"Well, well I would really say it has been, a week ago."*

Mfumu (Judge) - *Tailor, "Give a legitimate reason why you actually decided to wear that particular client's pants?"*

Answer (Tailor)- *"Well I was just curious to feel how this exclusive fabric feels on someone's body, but unfortunately I got caught by my client. He shrugged.*

Verdict - **The tailor obviously had lost the case, and was penalized, for breach of the contract. His penalty was, he had to pay two goats and two chickens plus two "Nkalu" or containers of palm wine, in order to meet the requirements of his Traditional law.**

Chapter VI

Communication Gap Between Modern and Traditional Law

CAN A VILLAGE CHIEF BE HELD ACCOUNTABLE BY HIS CONSTITUENTS FOR HAVING FAILED TO ADVICE THEM?

POOR COMMUNICATION AND FINANCE LOSS

Based on the Congolese traditional law, in some areas of Bandundu province in Luniungu region, a village chief is almost venerated by his constituents. It has always been so since the time of their ancestors.

When thinking of their Chief, the villagers evidently allude to the power, ability and the wisdom of the individual who has inherited that title of honor. And therefore, people have a high expectation of their chief's leadership. People look to their chief for any sudden change, which might occur in the course of the day, the week, or the year in and around the village or throughout the country.

They rely completely on their chief's wisdom in guiding and caring for them. In addition, they trust that any slightest, or unusual situation which might occur around their village or in the country in general would be addressed or announced by the chief, either to urge the people to act in appropriate manners, or to calm them down, in case of any uncertainty or disruption caused by vicious foreign individuals.

Unfortunately, during the current era, things do not seem to follow their regular routine as they have always been during the ancestors' time, *according to the villagers*. Apparently, certain village chiefs are becoming backslidden in terms of their responsibilities; perhaps due to the modern economic dilemma, and the pressure caused by the outsiders such as impostors, or the ferocious individuals.

Lately, in our modern time, the village chiefs had developed the habit of possessing a portable radio, which helps them to listen to the news broadcast, and subsequently, they would announce any changes which might suddenly affect his constituents.

Evidently, economic dilemma in any country affects practically everyone, even though the degree of that change may not be proportionate. Further, the communication gap among the people creates unnecessary confusions between them, especially when the means of communication is unreliable.

In Bandundu region for instance, and precisely in Luniungu region, the economic dilemma and lack of adequate communications had resulted to a terrible turmoil between the villagers and theirs chiefs, especially in one particular village. Although the village chief had been aware of the constant deflation and fluctuation of their national currency during that particular period of time, but it has been no implication to the change of the currency as far as the people were concerned.

Nevertheless, when the chief had least expected, and especially, for not keeping abreast with the national news for quite some time, he was ultimately taken by surprise. Spontaneously, the chief was informed after one month that due to the consecutive fluctuations of the country's currency, the government had decided to devalue the old currency; and that the new currency has been in effect since one month ago. It was also confirmed that the old currency would no longer be useful anywhere in the country. Currently, it has become worthless. And, therefore, anyone who is still holding the old currency might as well forget about it completely, and never to recall that they have money in their possession. It is void. It is good for nothing at the present time. The chief was dismayed, disturbed and frightened. How would he ever deliver such information to his people? Considering the fact that the banking institutions do not exist in the remote parts of the country, and particularly around the villages, people had always saved their money in their homes.

Further, due to the fact that the official Market in that area was being held only once a month, the village chief had faced a serious communication problem with his people indeed. Because the radio was the only means of communication for the chief to get the national information and share it with his people, but during that time, due to the dead batteries, the radio was not operating. There were no shopping centers nearby to acquire them immediately.

However the chief had planned to send someone to go and purchase the needed batteries on the next upcoming Market Day. At the Market, the eminent businessmen and customers originating from various areas, gather to conduct their commercial activities of diverse goods. Therefore, the village chief had expected to acquire les batteries on that day as well as other commodities, as usual.

Unfortunately, the awful news came prior to the Market Day, and therefore, the chief had been unable to listen to the news and also share it with his people on time. *What a disaster*! He had been unable to advise his constituents about converting their money to the new currency on time, due to the fact that the radio had not been functioning.

Certainly the national event actually had taken place during that time. Apparently it had been announced through the radio which was the only means of communication. The question asked, "If it had been really announced through the radio, but how long they kept that announcement on the air, which could have permitted every individual including those in remote parts of the country to hear and also allow the people to meet that obligation on time?"

In addition, the lack of adequate means of transportations would required more time to allow villagers to travel to different towns in order to meet with the potential businessmen or stores owners and request the money exchange services. The prominent local businessmen usually were known to be lenient in terms of the currency exchange, provided that it was being done within the time limit for that matter.

THE VILLAGERS' REACTION

When the news was reported by the traders, who had recently returned from different towns to conduct their respective businesses, they stated that the country's currency had just been devalued; the people could not comprehend it at first, what it actually meant. So in order to clarify the situation, those businessmen gave further simple explanation pertaining to their daily language, they said, "THE *OLD MONEY IS ACTUALLY DEAD*!" and that now the government has issued a new currency (*different kind of money to do business with*). This simply means, "*NEW TYPE OF MONEY*," they explained nervously to the villagers. Further, they displayed the different bills with the new denomination to the people who appeared perplexed.

Hearing this shocking and discouraging news, the entire village got excited. They became concerned, and everyone took out all their savings from their homes. Some farmers and others who conducted different kinds of trading used to save their money in the trunks or luggage, whereas the common people use to save their money in small containers.

Everyone was actually nervous, and began to place all their money outside of their homes, in front doors. Each one stood before his or her money, whining, "Now what shall we do with all this money, if the officials wind up refusing to exchange it?" People could hardly believe that their endeavors had actually been wasted. They were naturally disturbed. Mothers looking at their children's needs felt so badly.

Ultimately, they began crying for all the energy spent to produce all that money, which they actually needed to pay for their children tuitions, buy them school supplies, and uniforms. Now what is next? *People questioned.*

In addition, parents had developed the habit of supplying the school kids with daily allowance in order to help them buy "Mikate (donut)" or snack around the school during their break time. Also, their money was needed to make church contributions, so that they could continue to serve Nzambi-Mpungu (God Almighty) who watches over them and showers them with His Blessing of harvest. He allows them to get to Heaven after their earthly pilgrimage.

Obviously, parents were deeply concerned regarding their children's education, due to the fact that public schools are practically non-existent throughout the country. People were panic-stricken. They were actually in such a confused state of mind. And as a result, they started to run towards the village chief's residence for a possible solution. They were whining, while dragging all their money to the chief's home. Their frustration was actually directed towards their chief, for having failed in making announcements and advising his fellowman in taking any precautionary measures, as the African norms actually require; taking that approach would have allowed people to have their money exchanged in a timely manner. Now, under this circumstance, what is our alternative? *They questioned, angrily*.

THE VILLAGE CHIEF'S REACTION

The village chief was quite disturbed, nervous and frightened to face the people. He was very apologetic, and said repeatedly to his constituents, "I too, have plenty of money in my house." Thus, his family members immediately brought out a trunk full of money in order to prove to those individuals that the chief was innocent, and that he had no intention to trick or mislead them. He just had not been aware on time.

He said to the angry mob, "All of us are actually in the same boat. I apologize, as you know better, that it is naturally my responsibility to inform you of any slightest change that has suddenly occurred around us all. This dilemma is due to the fact that my portable radio had run out of batteries. I had attempted to expose them on the Sun, but they are completely dead and no transmission was received. I was looking forward to this upcoming Open Market Day in order to send my collaborator to go, and buy new batteries, but unfortunately, look what has just happened to all of us? This is very unfortunate to all of us indeed. After hearing the chief concern, their anger was now directed towards the Rulers or the nation, stating "They should have given the people at least two months or even three months in order to allow everyone to acquire the new currency!" *Are those leaders, impostors who have no knowledge of our ancestors' respect and integrity?*

People had obviously pronounced all kind of unkind words during that time. They brought forth words which would have never been pronounced otherwise. Evidently, those words were just heartbreaking to hear. People acted in that manner in order to express their frustrations. The villagers began saying it blatantly, "Our current leaders have actually no compunction for taking the wrong approaches against the mass of the people. They fail to realize that the world is not made out of the cream of the crop alone; the mass of the people deserves a minimum recognition as well, because we are all human beings!

The majority of people actually have no regret to act harshly towards others. Once they have been placed in a position of trust, apparently, they tend to forget where they came from. They rejoice exceedingly to view the miseries of others, until one day, they too would start reaping what they have sowed. *That was the discourse of one of the female clan leaders.* She actually spoke out without any reservation! The rest of the people supported her view, and then added, "Yes, yes, that is exactly what we have been noticing during this so *called modern time.* Our ancestors were always concerned for everyone's well being in the society, as opposed to the contemporary traditional law. They actually had resilience, and that was the reason why their social and political structures were well organized and stable, so to speak.

The chief had actually made an attempt to calm his constituents, who continued to carry on with complaints. Some people were standing by the chief's residence with their hands crossed over their heads, whereas others were holding their waists, whining. While other people had their arms crossed over their chest, and some were just heaving sighs and shaking their heads for such unacceptable event.

However, in order to ensure some consolation to his people, the chief decided to travel personally to the nearby local "Secteur" (*small government office*) in order to inquire whether or not they could possibly make any sort of adjustments to the villagers who were unable to exchange their money on time, due to the delay in receiving information or precise information?

Nevertheless, his meeting with the officials had not brought any positive results. According to the chief's report, those officials, appeared unconcerned and indifferent to the villagers' loss. However, when he had verified the information regarding the new currency which the officials had just introduced, the officials had confirmed the fact of having issued a new currency. The chief was also shown how those different new bills appeared to be. The chief pleaded to have mercy on his constituents including himself, due to the circumstance they have been in (lack of communication); He repeatedly begged them to bent a little, even though, they had fallen after the due date.

Further, he had pleaded, if they could actually be lenient, and allow the villagers to come by, and exchange all their money. The village chief was however told rudely, that *"They regret no adjustment was to be made. And that it was just too late to revise their decision."* They replied. The officials had shown no degree of compassion to the villagers. The chief pleaded, and explained the situation, repeatedly; and still, his endeavor had not been successful. Finally then, he asked, *"What were their implication in regard to this situation, and what should the people do with the old currency, which they have acquired laboring all their lives?"*

One agent replied with disparaging tone of voice, *"Well let them do whatever they actually wish to do with it. It is now worthless anyway!"* It was appalling to see a man who was heartless to the miseries of his fellow beings. In addition, the agent added, *"If I were a chief like you, I would have made sure to listen to the news closely, because my constituents depend completely on their chief's knowledge. Where have you really been during all that time? How is it that you are now appearing here sluggishly? Had you felt asleep? Was your wife afraid to wake you up, and listen to the news?"*

The village chief added that government officials at the Sector, spoke to me disparagingly, they sounded unethical. Apparently they sounded impostors based on their speech and lack of refinement. They had exemplified no respect in every word which was voiced, as opposed to our Bantu/Congolese compassion. In fact, one of them asserted bluntly, "We are very sorry, but there is nothing else we can possibly do to remedy your situation." The Chief reported that "Having heard all those stern, firm and negative answers, I shook my head with a deep regret, and then, I departed from the local government's office of the Sector, and walked back to the village to face the angry mop who awaited the arrival of their chief who had gone to plead for their cause."

Reportedly, the village chief returned crying along the road, and had tried to envisage the suitable means of addressing his people, and advising, if possible to just accept the loss which they had incurred, because it was beyond his control. *We acknowledge modern law has its place in our contemporary life, but being led by impostors and treasons does not give us any alternative.*

In reality, the chief was more concerned about his constituents' money than about his own. Above all, he was concerned about losing his people's trust and faith in him which fact could discredit his ancestors' legacy whose motive was to raise the standard of living of his people and protect their interests by contrasting with the objective of the impostors. In reality, the impostors' goal is to lead people astray, especially to create confusion by all means necessary in order to loot, to destroy human lives as well their social ideals. Additionally, impostors' goal is to instill wrong concepts in the society, conceal and stigmatized the people's values. Apparently, this man was also aware of his true role as a village chief, which is really to utilize the insight which was given to him by Nzambe (uhn-Zambah) their God in order to perceive things ahead thereby preventing any kind of dilemma, *according to his ancestral legacy.* In addition, he recalled that a village chief was empowered, and was not supposed to hedge or evade any questions, or situations, but embrace them all with authority until a pacific solution is obtained. He was aware that a chief is required being alert, dynamite, and strong, but not frail like King Nzinga-Nkuvu who had not followed the insight that Nzambe (uhn-Zambah) had offered him to perceive things ahead and also prevent African people's misfortune which began from 15th centuries and which seem to last perpetually

Fortunately, the village chief was also a believer in Nzambi-Mpungu (God Almighty), besides from his firm belief in his traditional law. He reported that as he had been traveling back to the village, because the meeting was unsuccessful, that made him depressed thereby he felt obligated to stop his bike every now and then in order to utter a little prayer; so that, God would have mercy on him, and especially to prevent the angry mob from rising against him, for having failed to communicate with his people in order to prevent that enormous loss.

He recalled the human nature under such circumstance would flare up, and would not want to accept the loss. He felt therefore helpless to resolve this situation as a human being and began to weep all the way back.

How the Power of God Had Been Able to Soothe the Hearts of the Angry Villagers Beyond the Village Chief's Control?

As soon as the chief had arrived in the village, his people perceived a gloomy appearance of him. As soon as he got off his bike, those who had approached him realized that he had red and bulging eyes. He projected a feeling of despair. That sad view was enough for the people to realize that the response from the officials had actually been unsatisfactory. Shortly thereafter, the chief had called a meeting to order, the session began immediately. The chief wept as he narrated his awful experience with the so called government officials at the local office who seemed unsympathetic, as opposed to the really Bantu/Congolese traditional law which is composed of the real elements of life such as integrity, love, compassion, justice, loyalty, peace and respect.

Thus, the staunch Christians of the village had assembled together realized *Nzambi-Mpungu alone could revamp that disastrous event,* and therefore, they were united in prayer in order to find a spiritual comfort which could only come from their Nzambi-Mpungu. Apparently, the elders of his church were empowered, a Pastor preached words of encouragement, which was desperately needed. It was actually quite a propos with the circumstance. The preacher's sermon was as follow: *"Why should we mourn for material things my beloved ones?"* We should remember that the Creator, who had given us the strength to produce all the money which we have just lost, is still **ALIVE** more than ever! He had told us that **GOLD AND SILVER** belong to him, and if we do sincerely believe in everyone of His words, we should therefore know that whatever is lost today, He, our God has the Power to actually replace it at no time; if everyone can only believe in Its Power!

Besides, God had never failed his children, but He tests them most of the time, as we have been reading in our Scripture. It would not take long for our God who is so powerful to manifest his Power in our daily activities. Children of God, just remember that, *"We still have a rich soil to produce crops. We still have our farms, our palm trees that continue to produce oil. Further, we still have the peanut needed to extract oil. Furthermore, we still have our cattle and our fish ponds and rivers flourished with various fishes. So, let us remain calm and continue to be grateful. Let us actually begin by counting the previous blessings received, because in some other parts of the Earth, some people do not have what we were given here. The only difference is that, those people utilize what they have got wisely.*

Those people from other societies actually have learned how to expand it; and they also share it with the common people; even though that share may not be proportionate, nevertheless, they do and that is how those individuals move forward successfully! *The word SHARING should be our motto; however, impostors ignore it, because they belong to barbarous societies which exemplify nothing but penury.*

We will begin working collectively in cultivating our crops as we have been trained by our great-grandparents. Let us therefore keep on realizing that everything animate and inanimate comes from our ***Nzambe/Nzambe-Mpungu/Mungu (our great Being God.)*** He does care for each one of His creatures, and He also will return to everyone, more than what we have just lost. So, people let us trust in our Creator and let us continue to persevere in faith, so that all treasons may be dismissed from the land of our ancestors for good; and all the impostors may be expelled overtly.

The preacher continued, "*It is very pathetic indeed to hear about those loved ones who had lost their lives out of frustration of not being able to have their money exchanged.* On the other hand, it *is painful for having worked so hard in gathering such a big amount of money, and not be able benefit from it.* Certainly, it is inacceptable for the bankers to tell the business people that just because you have arrived at the last minutes, *for example: out of 60,000 Fr.*, the bank can only exchange 10% *however the 54,000 Fr. should be taken from you* since the old currency has been devalued, there would be no need to keep it. The Pastors said, "It is appalling indeed to witness *such inhuman treatment, from our modern law. This means ignoring the practice of justice and integrity."* Nonetheless, regardless to this entire negative situation, do not be dismayed, **because whatever begins in this world has a beginning and an end.** Even though, certain individuals forget to realize it sometimes, but we should always remember that," said Pastor.

The preacher was just inspired and touched both spiritual and moral issues, *he said*, "This situation does not mean that we ought to act immorally to our neighbors in order to make a living. We will rather work as we have always done, and earn whatever we need, because whatever we deserve, and earn honestly will eventually serve us better. However, remember what our ancestors have instructed us, *"Whatever goods that have been obtained forcibly by trying to rationalize the motive behind it, will bring nothing but miseries in the future. This is referring to our famous word called "CURSE. We should not fail to realize that the word curse seems little and abstract, however it has a big impact in our lives. It knows how to connect with its own kind in order to balance out everyone's action in life. And therefore, do not be a part of evil, hoping that you could be exempt from it.*

Let us remember that our ancestors were loyal to each other, and we too, shall be likewise. We should actually follow after their footsteps. *Remember also that a looter cannot bring the goods he had acquired dishonestly to Heaven, for God does not need any earthly soiled things. Further, the looter cannot even carry the ill-gotten gains to hell, because the hell has plenty of its own miseries to deal with.* So let us learn to relax and continue to count our daily blessings. Above all, remember our ancestors' virtues, always. Further, teach the new generation to come how to remain focused on our Bantus' qualities and maintain those values in order to prevent them being concealed or stigmatized once again.

Furthermore, let us keep on evoking our Nzambe (our God) so that our modern rulers may envisage developing, and building many financial institutions throughout the country which would accommodate every citizen on time and avert the crisis such as the one we are experiencing currently.

Because a society cannot be made out of the cream of the crop alone, but the mass of the people must be needed, as well in order to make the society effective. Therefore, any clever ruler cannot neglect his constituent, because it is them who make him or her successful leader, this wisdom came from our ancestors. That is why they ensured Integrity, Justice, Peace and Respect. Our great grandparents knew *also that without the mass of the people, the role of a ruler is worthless.*" The preacher concluded his spontaneous and powerful message on that awful day. Everyone was comforted, the degree of their anger subsided, and the hope had re-appeared, *according to our oral traditions.*

On the following day, however, the chief had organized another meeting in the attempt to win the trust of his people. He offered them a cow. People ate and drank fresh coffee and palm wine, as they were accustomed. Eventually, they were morally uplifted, and were grateful to Nzambi-Mpungu (God, the Almighty) for having allowed an event which had brought people very close to Him. The word of God was actually sufficient to soothe everyone's grief. Shortly after that horrible event, people gradually resumed their daily routine faithfully, *according to our oral traditions.*

Because the people were ironically told to do whatever they had wished to do with the old currency, which had become eventually worthless, so, different people took different approaches. Somme people said to themselves, *"Due to the fact that the old currency has been pronounced **DEAD**, then let us just **burry** it."* So, they did it.

Further, the other individuals said to themselves, *"Well; let us just **burn** this old currency, since it is now worthless, so that it could rapidly return to dust where it came from."* And so they did it.

Whereas, another group of people said to themselves, *"Each event in the society or in the country makes the History of that society or the nation. And therefore, the new generation would need to actually see the proof of this awful event, when they will be studying the history of our society or our nation.* For that reason, they chose to nail some of those old bills on their walls. The rest of the bills were archived in the traditional containers for the purpose of educating the future generation, so that they would learn how to compare, or to contrast modern and traditional laws in terms of their efficiency. Thus, with respect to selecting their modern leaders, it would be preferable to place individuals who are anchored in the Bantu/Congolese traditions.

The later group thought it was necessary for the future leaders to be made aware of their main responsibilities towards their fellow beings and the need of establishing an effective communication with every individual of the different level. This would prevent the leaders from making similar mistake such as the current one where the village chiefs and modern leaders had failed to have a clear and courteous dialogue in order to assist the citizens in resolving their problems.

However, few months after that event, the Pastor was again inspired to preach on the need of the people at that particular time, his subject was, **"Forgiveness."** *His sermon was based on how to forgive and to forget completely anything that had occurred in the past, which has not brought you any joy.* He actually referred to the loss of people's savings, which has brought distress and a heartbreaking experience to all the villagers.

The preacher was quite aware that many individuals were still dwelling in that awful event, due to the fact that they have kept those old bills in their homes. He therefore convinced everyone to clean up their homes, and to let go completely of those old bills that kept on bringing back sad memories. The Pastor and the village Chief reminded the villagers that, "Our ancient Traditional Law has always been orally transmitted, and so shall be the contemporary Traditional Law. We cannot break the momentum, because today's events would add to the past history as far as the new generation is concerned.

CONCLUSION

Based on the Bantu genealogical information, the new generation is being orally informed by its great-grandparents that the Congolese political and economical systems during our ancestors' time have always been more efficient, because their currency remained strong and stable. Further, they had never experienced any fluctuation, deflation or inflation in their monetary or economic system. They were applying their God given wisdom.

And therefore, the youth are recommended to always refer to their ancestors' wisdom, because their society had known neither political nor economical instability prior to the foreigners' invasions, which had introduced the activities of the *"MUNDEL A BANGOMBE"* pronounced, *Mun-dal-ah-ban-gom-bah* (referring to the kidnappers of the Congolese people). *According to the oral traditions,* the genealogical information from ancestors revealed that the activities of the *MUNDEL A BANGOMBE* had generated families' resettlement from one part of the country to another part of the country, and also throughout the world. It had also been revealed that the Bantu/Congolese ancestors lived and traded harmoniously and peacefully with each other, prior to that misfortunate era. So, based on their loyalty, they were aware of how to network with others without meddling in their privacy, thereby respecting boundar.

Therefore, elements such as looting, impunity and corruption were foreign to them. In fact, they are known as being viciousness or crimes in their society, because the above mentioned elements were introduced by the impostors whose motive is to make profits by imposing depravity, destruction and impurity. However, during the ancient time their homes were always left open. Friends or acquaintances could get in and out at any time, and willfully with no harm. They could sit down and rest for a while, and then resume their journeys, shortly, thereafter. Hospitality was well practiced then. In fact, strangers could always be served whenever they were hungry or thirsty. Further, they could also be sheltered free of charge, as opposed to our contemporary time, apparently that is due to the viciousness caused by the impostors and treasons, throughout the land, which has thereby resulted to a high degree of apprehension between the people.

Ancestors had always had abundance to spare and surplus to store in their **MIKALA (mekalah) according to Le Munsong Tribe, meaning** granary or grain warehouse. In fact, the word shortage was actually foreign to them. The rulers were held accountable for their actions to their people. It was mandatory for village heads to ensure clear and precise communication with the constituents, because the people venerated their rulers and always followed their advices or directions.

Overall, in the Traditional law, as was previously indicated, words such as impunity, corruption, intrigues, and treachery are non-existent. Based on integrity and justice; nobody is placed above the law. *The Mfumu and Mbaku are always aware that the judgment is to be conducted under the eye of Nzambe (in Lingala language/Nzambi-*

Mpungu (in Kikongo language)/Mungu (in Swahili) - Meaning God, the Great Being in heaven, who can strike on his people if justice is not applied accordingly. So, **the verdict of any trial is to be given fairly; based on the logic, and following the sequence of the events involved.** In this way, God and the ancestors who had attended the judgment would be satisfied, because the people have honored them.

In essence, this is one of the reasons why the traditions are orally transmitted, because *certain elements relative to the core traditions are considered to be sacred. And therefore should only be divulged to the individuals who had been empowered, or enthroned based on the family's hierarchy, thereby preventing any sort of distortion.*

Therefore, in the Bantu/Congolese culture, usurpation of the village or families' power is regarded as a serious crime; and its repercussion is death or sentence in the local government's Court of law. Additionally, it is imperative that all the judges presiding the Bantu peoples' modern government offices be from the Bantu/Congolese culture that have the knowledge of both modern and traditional law combined in order to be able to conduct judgments accurately or efficiently. Currently, however, the natives of the Bantu/Congolese culture have developed a cynical attitude towards the colonials' information written regarding their traditions. In reality, people only believe in the facts obtained directly from their chiefs or the clan leaders who hold the knowledge of their Traditional law flawlessly. *And therefore, the rulers in the Bantu/Congolese society are required to be authentic, capable in ensuring and maintaining political and social stability in order to meet the ancestral requirements.*

The weakness of contemporary law is viewed in the fact that the leaders appear backslidden in terms of their leadership. Woman's authority and progress are smothered. Human rights and respect are violated. Further, the persistence of the instability in Economic and Monetary system; all the above situations are contributing to the dilemma of our contemporary society, which is quite opposite of the ancient Bantu/Congolese society.

In essence, even though the Bantu/Congolese "Traditional Law" is orally transmitted, it is however, accurate and efficient as far as the Congolese's culture is concerned. *Ultimately, our modern law holds its right place in our modern society, however it cannot replace, the*

Bantu/Congolese traditional law in terms of its firm beliefs in **Mibeko** *(me-bah-kou)* **Ya** *(yah)* **Ba** *(bah) Koko as it is called in Lingala language – and in Kikongo language it is referred to as:* **NSIKU** (*uhn-se-ku* **YA** (*ya*) **BA** (bah) **MBUTA** (*uhm-bu-tah*) **– This simply means the law of our ancestors, because the Bantu/Congolese *Traditional Law, in reality, encompasses the following elements: Loyalty, justice, integrity, love, peace, hospitality and respect, as well as the fear of Nzambe (the Great Being) and also, the respect to their ancestors.***

Conversely, the new generation keeps on questioning whether or not studying of someone's background is still necessary, in this day and age? We have always replied that, "Yes," it is vitally important to learn history, because knowing the origin of any entity would help us in clarifying and correcting the mistakes of the past thereby extracting the wisdom of the past which could help us to evolve effectively in terms of broadening our perspectives, as well as expanding our knowledge, in that respect, we can be able to build a strong foundation of our contemporary life.

FINIS

BEPONA BOOKS

Africa Presents

- The Congo RDC and Lingala Language (English and French version (First edition) - **LINGALA/ENGLISH AND FRENCH/LINGALA DICTIONARIES**

- The Congo RDC and Kikongo Language (English and French version (first edition). - **KIKONGO/ENGLISH DICTIONARY**

- The Congo RDC and Child Education (First edition)

- The Congo RDC and Congolese Cuisine (First edition)

- The Congo RDC and A Congolese Woman Chief (Mfumu-Mkento)

- The Congo RDC Et la Femme Dirigeante (Mfumu-Nkento)

- The Congo RDC and Congolese Tradition Law (first edition)

- The Congo RDC and Congolese Comedy/Novels

   1. A Mysterious Boy called Timo Mikwaya Well known as Kamina

   2. Mr. Aleyi-Atondi

      How can this man live with his In-laws for over 15 years?

   3. A Western Professor with an African University Student (Abelengezi)

   4. Experience of two African young ladies in America (Magoke)

   By

   Bepona Collection

Books' Samples

Africa presents the Congo RDC and A Congolese Woman chief (Mfumu-Nkento (**pronounced uhm-foomoo-kan-too**)

English  Français

Africa presents the Congo RDC and **Child Education in the Bantu society**

Africa presents the Congo RDC and **Congolese Cuisine**

Africa presents the Congo RDC and Lingala Language English French versions

Africa presents the Congo RDC and Kikongo ya l'Etat English and French versions

ABOUT BEPONA COLLECTION

The authors of BeponaBooks are female Congolese-American. We write about the culture of the Bantu society of the Congo RDC, which is located in Central Africa - (MPA, PAS, BBA, and BA).

In essence, our books are apolitical. They are based on our personal research conducted scholarly and confirmed by oral traditions of the Bantu peoples, transmitted to us by our live Historians. In fact, the live historians are the wise living senior citizens who continue to maintain and sustain the authenticity of the oral traditions without any distortion. Generally, we concentrate our books on presenting the Congolese culture, which encompasses general social issues. Evidently, our contemporary history is connected to our ancient traditions. And therefore, we cannot omit touching some other topics, although slightly-sometimes-when we write about Congolese's culture

Our readers will notice that the titles of all our books in English are prefaced with, "Africa Presents the Congo RDC," and then, are followed by the actual book titles. The titles of all our books in French are prefaced with, "L'Afrique Présente Le Congo RDC," and then, followed by the actual book titles. Actually, we purposely took this approach, because we realize that not everyone is proficient in Geography. Apparently, certain individuals still believe that Africa is a country rather than a Continent. It is therefore, necessary to clarify the fact that the Congo RDC is a country within this particular Continent and not the other way around.

In writing about the Bantu/Congolese culture, we opted to focus on the most important social topics, namely, "Traditional law (Common law), Congolese woman's leadership, Congolese cuisine, and Child education. We also have developed two major Congolese languages (Called Lingala and Kikongo ya l'Etat, that including their respective dictionaries. These languages are spoken in three or four other African countries.

All our books are written in simple terms, language and style. Our goal is to share our culture with individuals, who are interested in diversity, and to express ourselves, but not to impress our readers. Ultimately, in regard to the bibliography, we owe all our credits to the Bantu live historians from the Democratic Republic of the Congo RDC.

The picture illustrates three Village Chiefs in the Congo RD, dressed in their casual outfits while conducting an informal discussion.

There are three village chiefs in this picture. Chiefs are wearing special hats designed just for them. The rest of the individuals seated next to each chief are their collaborators.

Civil Court in the village

A crowd awaiting the arrival of jury to begin the Session

A crowd awaiting the arrival of jury to begin the Session

KINSHASA, THE CAPITAL CITY OF THE CONGO RDC
PRIOR TO THE CIVIL WAR

DEMOCRATIC REPUBLIC OF CONGO RDC

M A P

AFRICA

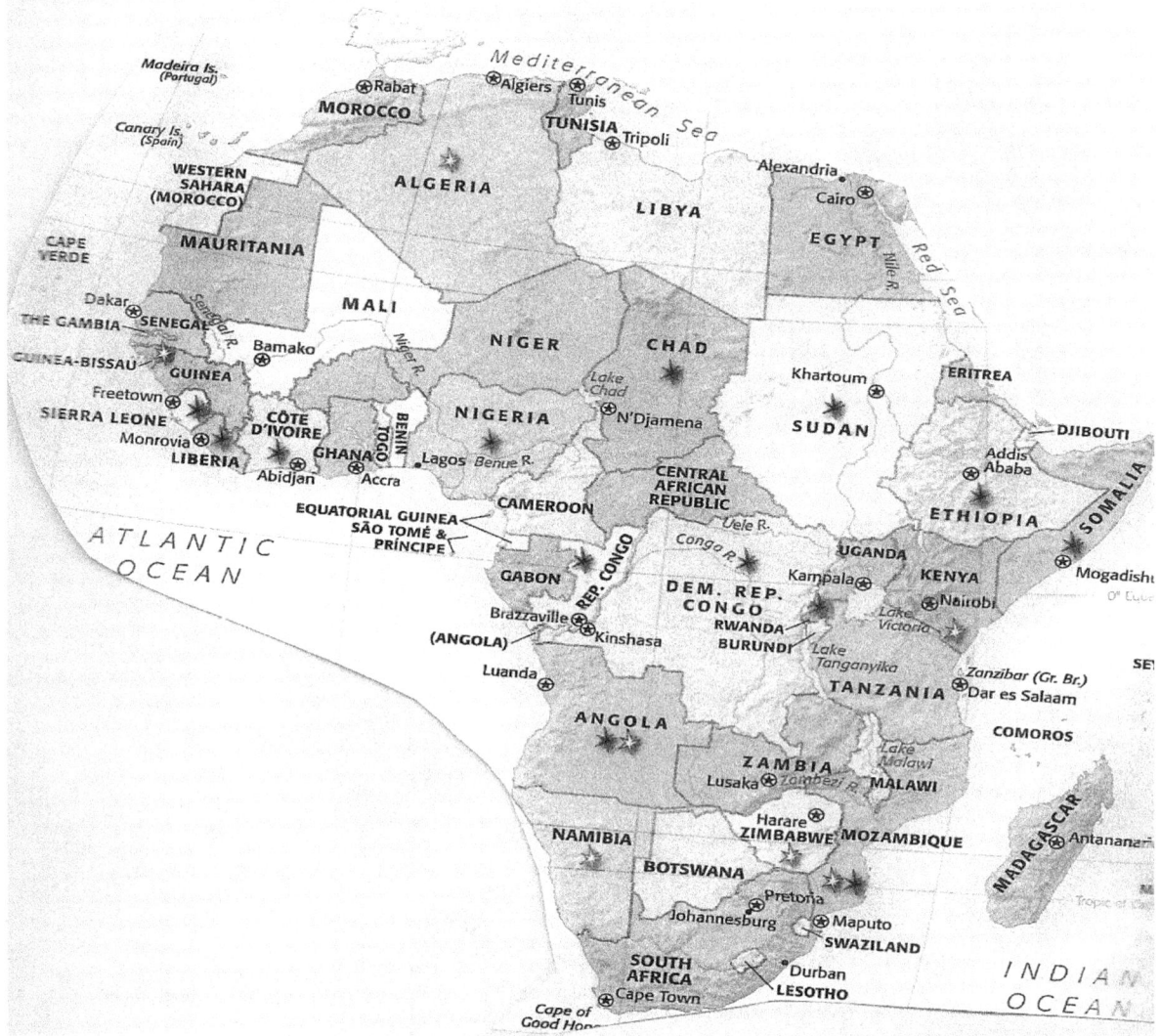

Index

V